Divinity

in

Leadership

Divinity in Governance

OKESOLA MOSES OLUSOLA

ISBN 979-8-88616-949-2 (paperback)
ISBN 979-8-88616-950-8 (digital)

Christian Faith Publishing
832 Park Avenue
Meadville, PA 16335
www.christianfaithpublishing.com

Printed in the United States of America

To the glory of God through Jesus Christ by whom I have found grace and acceptance to be called by His name.

But Jesus called them to him, and saith unto them, Ye know that they which are accounted to rule over the Gentiles exercise lordship over them, and their great ones exercise authority upon them. But so shall it not be among you; but whosoever will be great among you, shall be your minister; And whosoever of you will be chiefest, shall be servant of all. For even the Son of man came not to be ministered unto, but to minister, and to give his life a ransom for many.
—Mark 10:42–45

I am the good shepherd. The good shepherd lays down his life for the sheep.
—John 10:11

It is an abomination to kings to do evil, for the throne is established by righteousness.
—Proverbs 16:12

A ruler who lacks understanding is a cruel oppressor, but he who hates unjust gain will prolong his days.
—Proverbs 28:16

Moreover, look for able men from all the people, men who fear God, who are trustworthy and hate a bribe, and place such men over the people as chiefs of thousands, of hundreds, of fifties, and of tens.
—Exodus 18:21

Blessed are you, O land, whose king is of nobility and whose princes eat at the appropriate time—for strength and not for drunkenness.
—Ecclesiastes 10:17

Propitious smiles of heaven can never be expected on a nation that disregards the eternal rules of order and right, which Heaven itself has ordained.
—President George Washington

Contents

Author's Note

The Holy Bible is the reference book in all the scriptural quotations in this book, mostly from KJV.

Except where the character in this book is either a man or a woman, the use of *man*, *he*, *his*, and *him* in this book are for writing convenience; a man is also talking about a woman—it is also either he or she, and his/him or her.

Acknowledgment

I cannot help but appreciate the impact of the following mentors and spiritual fathers l have had in my life: Prophet Abel Olorunosebi (my late father), Dr. John Maxwell, Pastor Gideon Oyedepo, Bishop David Oyedepo, Papa Enoch Adeboye, Papa William Kumuyi, Dr. Myles Munroe (late), Papa Gbile Akanni, Emily Adewuni (my late mother and a moral leader), and a host of many unknown and uncelebrated generals in the camp of God whose lives and what they live for inspire me to press on for God.

My sincere appreciation goes to my amiable and submissive wife, Douye Felicia, and my wonderful son, Einstein Paul Oluwatimilehin, whose support and cooperation cannot be overemphasized in my journey toward the accomplishment of God's eternal purpose for my life.

I am also indebted to good people of Fruitful Hill Centre for their support and encouragement toward my position as resident pastor in their midst over the past ten years. Their commitment to God's kingdom business is astonishing.

Thank you all.

Introduction

L ife begets life; therefore, a man can only give what he has and possesses. Despite the exploits of men, they are restricted, limited, and constrained in all their wisdom, knowledge, research, and impacts.

The business of governing, leading, coordinating, directing, and organizing men is a complex one; no man in his common sense has what it takes to manage others alike because of their inherent complexities.

Man is too complex to administer; man's behavioral tendencies are unpredictable, his thoughts are unsearchable, and he lives sometimes with his head in disagreement with his heart. Above all, man is not crafted in the image of another man but God's.

The business of governing men at all levels of human management is that of God; only He made man, only He molded him, only He understands man, and in Him is available the ultimate wisdom and capabilities to lead men.

God is the potter, man is the clay, and the consciousness of men does not imply absolute knowledge of who they are; neither does it suggest that they are independent of their Maker.

The desire of a man is the reflection of his complexity coupled with ill-knowledge of several of his needs.

This inspired book is written to connect divinity and human government; it informs us that only God can bear absolute rule in the affairs of men, and only God's kind of leadership can meet the needs and aspirations of men.

Among critical issues in leadership vehemently discussed include: "The Theory of Man's Needs," "The Leaders of Men at this Time," "The Failure of Leadership," "God's Criteria for Leadership," "God's Choice of Leaders," "The Foolishness of God Revealed," "How to Divinely Govern Men," "The Wisdom from Above," "Raising Godly Generation," "The Core Responsibility of the Church of God," "Divinity upon the World System of Government," "31 Immutable Truths on Leadership," and "The Day of Reckoning."

Leadership!

The two legs of leadership are capacity and character; while capacity is the principal requirement, character is what sustains one in leadership. The leadership position a man occupies is strictly a function of the assignments or the purpose or the divine responsibilities the person is created for.

Therefore, leadership rests on a tripod of God's purpose for man, inherent and developed capacity in him/her, and godly character building.

Where there is gross deficiency in either capacity or character or both, the leader and the lead will end up far worse than where they were coming from, and eventually, the whole essence of leadership will be defeated.

There is no leader of repute in any part of the world that had led or is leading or that may emerge in the space of time triumphantly beyond the understanding he/she has about God's deliberate reason for his/her existence, his/her inmate gifts and talents, his/her burning passions, and his/her relationship with God.

There is no one created by God who is not responsible for at least one thing in life, and that implies everyone has a leadership role even though not every person would be in leadership position. It is the leadership role that makes every individual a leader, and not the position assigned to it.

There are many people who are in leadership position that have not passed the test of capacity and character requirements for leadership; they are the ones who are mostly in control of the leadership space across the world and, therefore, are disaster in every area to humanity. It is as a result of this experience that God gives details of who should be a leader in any respect in order to save the human race from total collapse and destruction.

The premise of leadership is to coordinate the affairs of men in a manner that allows order and discipline by defined or regulated conduct, human resource development and management, human influence, rebuke and correction, team-building, and defined positions on all human issues so as not to have unregulated preferences over the management of human complexity and its courses.

This premise of leadership is as the distance of heaven from the earth if allowed to be created or established by men, because the very best of a natural man born of a woman is the worst of it and is never sufficient to manage others. Therefore, no man has what it takes to provide leadership for others; every man is potentially endowed to be a type of leader and whom he/she intends to follow.

The management of the spirit, the soul, and the body of a man is of God who in turn endows men with the divine wisdom to rule others in their affairs.

However one sees it, leadership is more spiritual than reducing it to the business of sensual capacity and educational level; it is indeed a divine business and responsibility of some men for the sake of others.

> Leadership is a divine business and responsibility of some men for the sake of others. (Okesola Moses Olusola)

You are not a leader because you are in a leadership position, but you are if you have become a determinant of what others will do and what they might not do. Every man has a trait of a leader because all men are made by God, the first before all things and the commander to whom all creatures and creations oblige to.

While there are many schools of thought on *leadership*, the greatest book and revelation on leadership and leaders is the *Bible*, the Book of Life. The Bible gives detailed accounts of different leaderships and leaders, including the choices of men and that of God.

The Bible exposes even the wrongdoings of God's choice of leaders and what befell them because of their mistakes, errors, and disobedience to God's leadership tenets and principles.

This book draws unparalleled revelations and insights from the Bible to connect divinity to governance, and advances men's submission to God's teachings, principles, and instructions on leadership before they can enjoy the fullness of God's provision in peace at all times.

The Theory of Man's Needs Review

> Leadership is about meeting the needs of men, but these needs are insatiable and not within the power of any leader to satisfy; only God who made all things has unlimited capacity to surpass their provisions.

Maslow's Theory (1943) of individual development and motivation describes men as wanting beings who are never satisfied with what they have but desire more and more irrespective of what they earlier possessed. Maslow discovered that what men want depends on what they already have; he cascaded the needs of men in hierarchical manner as indicated below in the order of importance:

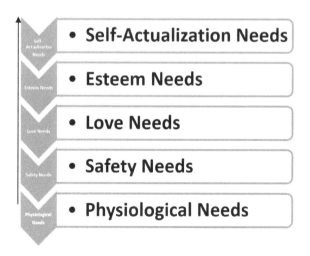

- Self-Actualization Needs
- Esteem Needs
- Love Needs
- Safety Needs
- Physiological Needs

Physiological Needs

What constitute these needs, according to Maslow, include satisfaction of hunger and thirst, and the need of regulated airflow in and out of the body at a required temperature. They also include shelter, sensory pleasures, power of influence, and sexual satisfaction.

Safety Needs

These include safety and security, freedom from pain or threat to life physically, protection from danger or deprivation, and the need for predictability and orderliness.

Love Needs

Which is termed social needs, such as being shown affection, sense of belonging, social activities, friendships, and both the giving and receiving of love.

Esteem Needs

Often referred to as ego needs which includes self-respect that involves desire for confidence, strength, independence, freedom, achievement, and esteem of others (which involves reputation or privilege, status, recognition, attention, and appreciation).

Self-Actualization Needs

Putting all resources at his disposal to actualize his/her dreams and aspirations as well as realizing and transforming his full potentials to results and accomplishments. Maslow sees this need as "must-be" or "becoming everything one is capable of becoming.'

The Maslow theory of needs seems to have expressed the needs of men, as believed by many; but one question on this theory is that, What degree of research sampling informed Maslow's conclusion?

I want to believe that Maslow's theory of human needs must have been based on a study of a particular group of people over a particular period of time, which would not have necessarily taken into consideration all categories of men at that time based on races, culture, environment, beliefs, behavioral patterns, and other tangible and intangible factors inherent in humanism.

There are many unknown needs of man which he never thought of, and very many times, man is faced with problem of misplaced priorities of needs. Therefore, "However efficient and effective a man can be, he knows only what he knows about himself but what he knows not he will never consider and think about. There are many unknown needs of man, and until he discovers them, such needs are never in his priority list" (Okesola Moses Olusola).

Man does not know everything about himself, but God knows. To restrict the needs of a man to what Maslow's theory captured is like building a model with an assumption that several factors are negligible, inconsequential, and tend to zero. The implication of the assumption on the model above is that the needs of man are not dynamic.

Analyzing Maslow's theory not to have justified the complexity of man is as follows:

❖ There are some needs that are low, lower, and lowest-level needs; and others are high, higher, and highest-level needs.
❖ No two people are the same in needs, capability, attitude, ability, character, etc.
❖ Individual differences mean that people place different values in the same need, which is to say, some people may consider higher-level needs of others as lower-level needs.
❖ There is a doubt about the time which elapses between the satisfaction of a lower-level need and the emergence of a higher-level need.

In all the above views, it can be inferred that the nature of man cannot be totally expressed in any form, the behavior of a man at times is unpredictable, the way of a man is unstable, and his uniqueness is shrouded in complexity.

> However conscious a man is to his needs and striving in life to meet them, he is still limited by reasoning and therefore, he remains unsatisfied even when certain needs have been met.

We can also justify the complexity of man by the interactions that exist among various activities in his natural space and spiritual space. Transmitting from one state to another is permeated by higher dimension of unknowns, imprecision, and uncertainties.

There has not been any theory propounded that captures the completeness of what, how, and where requirements pertain to a man's needs, but the Bible does.

A man sometimes behaves without being able to offer an explanation why he did what he has done. The scientific studies confirmed a man to be a warm-blooded animal but who also consume cold-blooded animals; he is a specie that can lose his warmness in the period of coldness.

The desperate search by men for satisfaction is noticeable in our day-to-day attempt to survive. Those who have not become established run the race of life to do so, those who are enjoying at some levels are dreaming of moving higher, and the ones who have lost their comfort at a particular time are doing all they can to recover.

Despite all efforts by men to reposition their lives, satisfactions have never been met or say their urge for more increases. Therefore, meeting the needs of men is beyond them. It is the Lord's; He alone knows a man's end from his beginning—He knows how to satisfy man, when to satisfy him, and where.

Psalmist writes in Psalm 23:

> *The LORD is my shepherd; I shall not want. He maketh me to lie down in green pastures: he leadeth me beside the still waters. He restoreth my soul: he leadeth me in the paths of righteousness for his name's sake.*

Yea, though I walk through the valley of the shadow of death, I will fear no evil: for thou art with me; thy rod and thy staff they comfort me[4]. Thou preparest a table before me in the presence of mine enemies: thou anointest my head with oil; my cup runneth over. Surely goodness and mercy shall follow me all the days of my life: and I will dwell in the house of the LORD for ever.

Psalmist was deeper in explaining that only God knows in absolute term the needs of men, and only He can provide them.

Be not ye therefore like unto them: for your Father knoweth what things ye have need of, before ye ask him... Therefore take no thought, saying, What shall we eat? Or, What shall we drink? Or, Wherewithal shall we be clothed? (For after all these things do the Gentiles seek:) for your heavenly Father knoweth that ye have need of all these things. (Matthew 6:8, 31–32)

Let us therefore come boldly unto the throne of grace that we may obtain mercy, and find grace to help in time of need. (Hebrews 4:16)

But my God shall supply all your need according to his riches in glory by Christ Jesus. (Philippians 4:19)

What men termed to be their needs are mostly materials in nature, but their largest number of needs is immaterial. Hebrews 10:36 says: *"For ye have need of patience, that, after ye have done the will of God, ye might receive the promise."* The need analysis of men has been captured and measured on mostly material basis, but in the real sense of what men should have need of, they are better diagnosed and measured spiritually.

A man is a spiritual being whose needs for existence and sustenance are mostly intangible, and only God can meet those needs absolutely.

These needs differ from time to another time, age to another age, season to another season, etc. A man's needs sometimes are constrained by factors beyond his control and get more complicated when his needs have to be shared to the advantage of other people.

While the consciousness of individuals varies to their needs, the pot cannot know better than the potter. How to make it good, better, and best is the exclusive responsibility of the potter. Sometimes a man may know his needs, but how to meet them is shrouded and clouded in darkness. *The three connectors of a path to meeting a need is: what is needed, when is it needed, and how to meet the needs.*

Only God knows the needs of men, when the needs are required, and how to meet them. The Bible says:

> *Ask, and it shall be given you; seek, and ye shall find; knock, and it shall be opened unto you: For every one that asketh receiveth; and he that seeketh findeth; and to him that knocketh it shall be opened. Or what man is there of you, whom if his son ask bread, will he give him a stone? Or if he ask a fish, will he give him a serpent? If ye then, being evil, know how to give good gifts unto your children, how much more shall your Father which is in heaven give good things to them that ask him?* (Matthew 7:7–11)

> *But when ye pray, use not vain repetitions, as the heathen do: for they think that they shall be heard for their much speaking. Be not ye therefore like unto them: for your Father knoweth what things ye have need of, before ye ask him.* (Matthew 6:7–8)

No man can meet the needs of others except if it is giving from above. God gave them manna in the wilderness:

> *And the mix multitude that was among them fell a lusting: and the children of Israel also wept*

again, and said, "Who shall give us flesh to eat?
We remember the fish, which we did eat in Egypt
freely; the cucumbers, and the melons, and the
leeks, and the onions, and the garlic: But now our
soul is dried away: there is nothing at all, beside
this manna, before our eyes." And the manna was
as coriander seed, and the colour thereof as the
colour of bdellium. And the people went about, and
gathered it, and ground it in mills, or beat it in a
mortar, and baked it in pans, and made cakes of
it: and the taste of it was as the taste of fresh oil.
(Numbers 11:4–8)

He provided drinkable water from the rock:

"Behold, I will stand before thee there upon
the rock in Horeb; and thou shalt smite the rock,
and there shall come water out of it that the people
may drink." And Moses did so in the sight of the
elders of Israel. (Exodus 17:6)

He immuned them against sicknesses and diseases in the wilderness for forty years:

And I have led you forty years in the wilderness:
your clothes are not waxen old upon you, and thy shoe
is not waxen old upon thy foot. (Deuteronomy 29:5)

God provided the ram for Abrahamic sacrifice:

And Abraham lifted up his eyes, and looked,
and behold behind him a ram caught in a thicket
by his horns: and Abraham went and took the ram,
and offered him up for a burnt offering in the stead
of his son. (Genesis 22:13)

He made clothes of animal skin for Adam and Eve:

> *Unto Adam also and to his wife did the LORD God make coats of skins, and clothed them.* (Gen 3:21)

He provided water in the wilderness for Hagar and her son, Ishmael:

> *And Abraham rose up early in the morning, and took bread, and a bottle of water, and gave it unto Hagar, putting it on her shoulder, and the child, and sent her away: and she departed, and wandered in the wilderness of Beersheba. And the water was spent in the bottle, and she cast the child under one of the shrubs. And she went, and sat her down over against him a good way off, as it were a bowshot: for she said, "Let me not see the death of the child." And she sat over against him, and lift up her voice, and wept. And God heard the voice of the lad; and the angel of God called to Hagar out of heaven, and said unto her, "What aileth thee, Hagar? Fear not; for God hath heard the voice of the lad where he is. Arise, lift up the lad, and hold him in thine hand; for I will make him a great nation." And God opened her eyes, and she saw a well of water; and she went, and filled the bottle with water, and gave the lad drink.* (Genesis 21:14–19)

God did not allow the health of Moses, Methuselah, and host of them to fail:

> *And Moses was a hundred and twenty years old when he died: his eye was not dim, nor his natural force abated.* (Deuteronomy 34:7)

And all the days of Methuselah were nine hundred sixty and nine years: and he died. (Genesis 5:27)

And said, if thou wilt diligently hearken to the voice of the Lord thy God, and wilt do that which is right in his sight, and wilt give ear to his commandments, and keep all his statutes, I will put none of these diseases upon thee, which I have brought upon the Egyptians: for I am the Lord that healeth thee. (Exodus 15:26)

And he healed many that were sick of divers diseases, and cast out many devils; and suffered not the devils to speak, because they knew him. (Mark 1:34)

He gave Hannah and Elizabeth children:

Wherefore it came to pass, when the time was come about after Hannah had conceived, that she bare a son, and called his name Samuel, saying, Because I have asked him of the LORD. (1 Sam 1:20)

But the angel said unto him, "Fear not, Zacharias: for thy prayer is heard; and thy wife Elisabeth shall bear thee a son, and thou shalt call his name John. And thou shalt have joy and gladness; and many shall rejoice at his birth." (Luke 1:13–14)

He provided a wife for Isaac:

And Rebekah lifted up her eyes, and when she saw Isaac, she lighted off the camel. For she had said unto the servant, "What man is this that walketh in the field to meet us?" And the servant had said, "It is my master:" therefore she took a veil, and covered herself. And the servant told Isaac all things that he had done. And Isaac brought her into his mother Sarah's tent, and took Rebekah, and she became his wife; and he loved her: and Isaac was comforted after his mother's death. (Genesis 24:64–67)

He fed Elijah by a raven and an angel:

> *And as he lay and slept under a juniper tree, behold, then an angel touched him, and said unto him, Arise and eat. And he looked, and, behold, there was a cake baken on the coals, and a cruse of water at his head. And he did eat and drink, and laid him down again. And the angel of the LORD came again the second time, and touched him, and said, 'Arise and eat; because the journey is too great for thee.' And he arose, and did eat and drink, and went in the strength of that meat forty days and forty nights unto Horeb the mount of God.* (1 Kings 19:5–8)

> *And the word of the LORD came unto him, saying, Get thee hence, and turn thee eastward, and hide thyself by the brook Cherith, that is before Jordan. And it shall be, that thou shalt drink of the brook; and I have commanded the ravens to feed thee there. So he went and did according unto the word of the LORD: for he went and dwelt by the brook Cherith, that is before Jordan. And the ravens brought him bread and flesh in the morning, and bread and flesh in the evening; and he drank of the brook.* (1 Kings 17:2–7)

He delivered a Zarephath-widow out of poverty:

> *And Elijah said unto her, Fear not; go and do as thou hast said: but make me thereof a little*

cake first, and bring it unto me, and after make for thee and for thy son. For thus saith the LORD God of Israel, The barrel of meal shall not waste, neither shall the cruse of oil fail, until the day that the LORD sendeth rain upon the earth. (1 Kings 17:13–14)

He rescued the sons of the prophets from debt:

Now there cried a certain woman of the wives of the sons of the prophets unto Elisha, saying, Thy servant my husband is dead; and thou knowest that thy servant did fear the LORD: and the creditor is come to take unto him my two sons to be bondmen. And Elisha said unto her, "What shall I do for thee? tell me, what hast thou in the house?" And she said, "Thine handmaid hath not any thing in the house, save a pot of oil." Then he said, "Go, borrow thee vessels abroad of all thy neighbours, even empty vessels; borrow not a few. And when thou art come in, thou shalt shut the door upon thee and upon thy sons, and shalt pour out into all those vessels, and thou shalt set aside that which is full." So she went from him, and shut the door upon her and upon her sons, who brought the vessels to her; and she poured out. And it came to pass, when the vessels were full, that she said unto her son, "Bring me yet a vessel. And he said unto her, There is not a vessel more. And the oil stayed." (2 Kings 4:1–6)

He gave children to women without wombs; He changed peoples' genotypes from SS to AA; He raised those who were already dead; He made a lame to work; He made a way on the sea; He heals nations of their woes and saved the world from damnation and destruction to come by ultimate sacrifice of His son, Jesus Christ, our Lord.

> *For God so loved the world, that he gave his only begotten Son, that whosoever believeth in him should not perish, but have everlasting life.* (John 3:16)

Because the needs of men are infinitesimal and many of them unknown to them, it is God that rules in the affairs of the kingdom of men; Only He knows their frailty and what it takes to continuously make available what they need.

> A man reasons to meet his needs within the scope of what is possible because many things are indeed impossible unto him, but to God all things are very possible.

Every need of a man requires give and take, and Jesus Christ gave His life so that all the needs of men can be met.

> *For God so loved the world that he gave his only begotten Son, that whosoever believeth in him should not perish, but have everlasting life.* (John 3:16)

> *In him was life; and the life was the light of men.* (John 1:4)

> *But Jesus beheld them, and said unto them, "With men this is impossible; but with God all things are possible."* (Matthew 19:26)

> *But my God shall supply all your need according to his riches in glory by Christ Jesus.* (Philippians 4:19)

The Leaders of Men at This Time!

> We are witnessing a world where most lead-
> ers are blind leading the blind; spiritually deaf and
> dumb struggling to communicate with others.

One important pillar that tells of what becomes of men's existence and sustenance is the leadership provided for them. Providing for the need of men is tied to their leadership. A leader provides direction; he knows what others do not; he creates the way to go and how to meet their needs.

However you see it, the destiny of men is tied to the leadership provided for and by them. A servant cannot be greater than leadership he yields himself to follow.

Therefore, meeting the needs of men at every sphere of life is tied to the leaders over them. It is consistent with God to raise leaders whose responsibilities are to provide leadership required by God to meet their needs.

The transitional flow to meeting people's need by God is as follows:

GOD'S KIND OF LEADERSHIP [LEADERS]

THE NEEDS OF MEN

GOD

We are not talking about human-crafted leadership, but God's type of leadership provided as the critical requirement in meeting the needs of all men. It is true that leaders that are from God are the provision to solve all diverse problems that are characterizing our world, but those leaders are also chosen by men. God does not impose a leader; it is the responsibility and choice of men to search a leader out.

The Scriptures say, *"When the righteous are in authority, the people rejoice: but when the wicked beareth rule, the people mourn"* (Proverbs 29:2).

Every space occupied by men is under a type of leader. There is a need for leadership in the communities, in the cities, in the rural places, in the families, in the nations, at schools, at worship centers, at public places, at private places, at local government levels, at state levels, at federal government levels, and every sector of the economy.

> Leadership constitutes a greater part of human institution and development; therefore, it is the critical path of what becomes of humanity.

The acceptable leaders of men at this time all over the world are those termed to be democratically elected by majority of a population even if the process is compromised without knowledge of the electorates.

Some leaders emerge because it is their families' right by history; some leaders emerge by appointment based on certain criteria which may not necessarily be stringent. Some find themselves in leadership by coercion, money influence, lies and propaganda, etc.

Terminologies like "equal right," "equal representation," "quota system," "political appointment," "technocrat appointees," "party slots," "women's right," "ethnic and religious consideration," "constituency representation," "political godfatherism," "inner caucus," "succession plan," etc. are buzzwords that are rending the leadership space across nations of the world.

> One shocking revelation in today's world is that the ungodly men are not just leaders almost

everywhere but are the deciders of who is fit for leadership.

Globally speaking, the best accepted form of leadership is through democracy, but this is not totally true in how God's kind of leaders emerge. The human democratic norm is full of manipulations, deceits, lies, cajoling, rigging, coercion, wickedness, hypocrisy, boss-servant relationship, unbridled appetite, and all manners of evil.

God's choice of men for leadership is strict, rigorous, faultless, and impartial, and above all, it follows after the pattern of the chief leader (Jesus Christ) of all men.

> *"For my thoughts are not your thoughts, neither are your ways my ways," saith the* LORD. (Isaiah 55:8)

> *For unto us a child is born, unto us a son is given: and the government shall be upon his shoulder: and his name shall be called Wonderful, Counselor, The mighty God, The everlasting Father, The Prince of Peace. Of the increase of his government and peace there shall be no end, upon the throne of David, and upon his kingdom, to order it, and to establish it with judgment and with justice from henceforth even for ever. The zeal of the* LORD *of hosts will perform this.* (Isaiah 9:6–7)

There were times in the Bible when kings Ahab and Jehoshaphat, kings Jehoram and Jehoshaphat seek to know the thoughts of God whether to go to a battle or not. But alas, four hundred prophets who provided spiritual leadership for Ahab at different times and places confirmed their victory. Prophets Micaiah and Elisha spoke the mind of God and prophesized about their defeat. (1 Kings 22:1–23; 2 Kings 3:5–12)

> *But it came to pass, when Ahab was dead, that the king of Moab rebelled against the king of Israel.*

And king Jehoram went out of Samaria the same time, and numbered all Israel. And he went and sent to Jehoshaphat the king of Judah, saying, "The king of Moab hath rebelled against me: wilt thou go with me against Moab to battle?" And he said, "I will go up: I am as thou art, my people as thy people, and my horses as thy horses." And he said, "Which way shall we go up?" And he answered, "The way through the wilderness of Edom."

*So the king of Israel went, and the king of Judah, and the king of Edom: and they fetched a compass of seven days' journey: and there was no water for the host, and for the cattle that followed them. And the king of Israel said, "Alas! That the L*ORD *hath called these three kings together, to deliver them into the hand of Moab!" But Jehoshaphat said, "Is there not here a prophet of the L*ORD*, that we may enquire of the L*ORD *by him?" And one of the king of Israel's servants answered and said, "Here is Elisha, the son of Shaphat, which poured water on the hands of Elijah." And Jehoshaphat said, "The word of the L*ORD *is with him." So the king of Israel and Jehoshaphat and the king of Edom went down to him.* 2 Kings 3:5–12

How democratic is God? His form of democracy is not a game of numbers; Micaiah versus other four hundred prophets is not a democratic ratio. God does not and will never go with majority, except the majority decides to go with Him.

> God does not and will never go with majority except the majority decides to go with Him.

Numerical strength is not a requirement for the choice of leaders by God, and neither does God allow emotions to permeate His thought process of raising a leader for His people.

One could attest to the fact that developed worlds have succeeded in arriving at leadership that are fairer than third-world countries but in the heart of leadership; it is not all about how leaders emerge and how fair the process of their emergence is but *what kind of leaders God called them.*

In most cases, what God called the crops of leaders being celebrated at this time are brooks of vipers. The world system in political, religious, business, and family spaces are led by criminals; the immoral; the ungodly; the wicked; liars; the unsaved; the unrighteous; and justice perverters, among many others. The world's leadership criteria are devoid of godliness, righteousness, and holiness which are central to God's choice of leaders.

> The world as it is today runs with a philosophy that separates leadership at all levels from godliness.

The body of knowledge over the years has identified types of organizations as the big factor for types of leadership. There have been traditional types of organizations where customs and long-standing beliefs are the basis for leadership authority.

In the *charismatic organizations*, the structure and capacity of authority is derived from personal qualities of a leader. This type of organization is at the mercy and wrath (feelings and emotions) of the leader; whatever he says is final.

Bureaucratic organizations are the other types where leadership authority is established on the basis of formal rules and procedures. These rules and procedures are built over a long period of time as the organization concerns evolves.

Whether an organization is classified as economic, protective, associative, public, service, and religious ones, people deserve the kind of leaders that lead them.

In leadership schools of thoughts, there have been trait theories that only consider personal qualities and characteristics very similar to what is obtainable in a charismatic organization. Among such leaders in history include Margret Thatcher (former UK prime minister), Nelson Mandela (former president of South Africa), Richard Branson (owner of Virgin Atlantic Airline), Steve Job (former president of Apple Computers), Ken Chenault of American Express, etc.

Research that goes back to 1930s to differentiate between leaders and non-leaders by virtue of their traits led to a review of twenty different studies of leadership traits. At the end, the result shows that five of the leadership traits considered was only common to four studies.

The interpretation of the scientific research shows that trait theories of leadership could not significantly establish a difference between effective and non-effective leaders.

> There is a very high tendency for a leader to be charismatic, enthusiastic, courageous, and still be morally bankrupt.

There have been propounded theories of leadership: such as *behavioral theories* which uses certain behavior metrics to differentiate between a leader and a non-leader; *contingency theories*, such as Fiedler Contingency Model, which affirm effectiveness in leadership as a result of a correct and situational match between a leader's style of interacting with subordinates/or people and what leadership situation demands at every point in time.

One powerful woman in history, Linda Wachner, CEO of Warnaco (an apparel company) in 1987—over a fourteen-year period—transformed Warnaco from a $425 million a year turnover to $12.2 billion organization but, in June 2001, was fired. The organization became bankrupt, and all she succeeded in were eroded.

Her leadership style that made her to be named America's most successful businesswoman in 1993 did not work for her in the year 2000 situations and circumstances.

One other theory of leadership in literature is *cognitive resource theory*. This theory focused on the intelligence and experience of a leader as a panacea to deal with stress that unfavorably affects performance in all ramifications.

But in all these theories, men are bound to fail; their strength can fail them and may not realize their expectations—even sometimes their strategies might not work for all situations.

> The leadership dynamics is a function of many variables that may be tangible or intangible, deterministic or continuous, precise or imprecise, certain or uncertain, discrete or dynamic, risky or non-risky, etc.

Though an effective leader's perception can be sufficient to deal with known and unknown leadership constraints, a leader is limited and is not sufficient in himself/herself.

> Every leader is limited and not sufficient in himself/herself.

I have concluded that even though leadership is a requirement for providing for and taking care of any situational and circumstantial needs, the best of human leadership can never be compared to God's choice of men in leadership.

> The best of human leadership can never be compared to God's choice of men in leadership.

> *Behold, thou art called a Jew, and restest in the law, and makest thy boast of God, And knowest his will, and approvest the things that are more excellent, being instructed out of the law; And art confident that thou thyself art a guide of the blind, a light of them which are in darkness, An instructor of the foolish, a teacher of babes, which hast the form of knowledge and of the truth in the law.*

> *Thou therefore which teachest another, teachest thou not thyself? Thou that preachest a man should*

not steal, dost thou steal? Thou that sayest a man should not commit adultery, dost thou commit adultery? Thou that abhorrest idols, dost thou commit sacrilege? For the name of God is blasphemed among the Gentiles through you, as it is written. (Romans 2:17–24)

Eli was the chief priest at a time in Israel and by divine providence; his children were also called the priests of the Lord. Eli followed tradition that automatically made his sons to be judges in Israel, but they eventually became a thorn in the flesh of all Israelites.

God's pronouncement by divine providence did not rubber-stamp Hophni and Phineas (Eli's sons) as priests of the Lord; they were not qualified in the first place since Eli knew their antecedent as ill-behaved children.

Eli ignored the godly criteria for priesthood and traditionally exalted his children to priesthood position; I will say that Eli imposed his children on Israelites. People revered Hophni and Phineas as priests of the Lord, but God called them sons of Belial which, by interpretation, means "sons of the devil."

Now the sons of Eli were sons of Belial; they knew not the LORD. *And the priests' custom with the people was, that, when any man offered sacrifice, the priest's servant came, while the flesh was in seething, with a flesh hook of three teeth in his hand;*

And he struck it into the pan, or kettle, or caldron, or pot; all that the flesh hook brought up the priest took for himself. So they did in Shiloh unto all the Israelites that came thither. Also before they burnt the fat, the priest's servant came, and said to the man that sacrificed, Give flesh to roast for the priest; for he will not have sodden flesh of thee, but raw.

And if any man said unto him, "Let them not fail to burn the fat presently, and then take as much as thy soul desireth; then he would answer him,

> *Nay; but thou shalt give it me now: and if not, I*
> *will take it by force."*
> *Wherefore the sin of the young men was very*
> *great before the LORD: for men abhorred the offering*
> *of the LORD.* (1 Sam 2:12–17)

At a time also in Israel when God rejected King Saul because of his flagrant disobedience and abuse of office as king over Israel, God commanded Prophet Samuel to anoint a teenager (David) in his place. Unfortunately, Prophet Samuel mistakenly wanted to anoint Eliab because of his physical personality, but God rebuked Samuel.

> *And Samuel did that which the LORD spake,*
> *and came to Bethlehem. And the elders of the town*
> *trembled at his coming, and said, Comest thou*
> *peaceably? And he said, "Peaceably: I am come to*
> *sacrifice unto the LORD: sanctify yourselves, and*
> *come with me to the sacrifice." And he sanctified*
> *Jesse and his sons, and called them to the sacrifice.*
>
> *And it came to pass, when they were come,*
> *that he looked on Eliab, and said, "Surely the*
> *LORD's anointed is before him. But the LORD said*
> *unto Samuel, "Look not on his countenance, or on*
> *the height of his stature; because I have refused him:*
> *for the LORD seeth not as man seeth; for man looketh*
> *on the outward appearance, but the LORD looketh*
> *on the heart." (1 Sam 16:4–7)

God does not choose leaders based on what the world considers most of the time, and that is why leadership at almost all levels at this time is failing and will continue to fail as long as men are not ready to accept godly criteria for leadership.

The Scriptures give accounts of leadership of many people in the Bible which are reality of leadership in our world today.

The Jeroboam's leadership (1 Kings 11:25–40); the Joash's leadership (2 Kings 12:1–15); the reign of Pharaoh at the time Joseph was in Egypt (Genesis 39–41); the rulership of King Nebuchadnezzar (Daniel 1–4); Eli and Samuel parenthood leadership (1 Sam 1, 2, 3, 7, 8); the leadership of King Herod of Judea at the time Jesus Christ was born (Matthew 2); the Haman's leadership (Esther 3–4); Jezebel and Ahab reign in Israe l(1 Kings 16–22; 2 Kings 9); and the compromised prophetic call of Balam (Numbers 22–24).

The Athaliah motherhood leadership (2 Kings 8:26–27); the pharisees and Sadducees' season of leadership (Matthew 3, 16, 19, 22, 23); the leadership provided by the ten spies in Israel excluding Caleb and Joshua (Numbers 13–14); King Saul's leadership (1 Samuel 9, 10, 13, 15–17, 19–23); the Abrahamic leadership (Genesis 11–25); and King David's leadership (1 Samuel 16–18; 2 Samuel 7–24).

The chronicles of the kings across many nations in the Bible (1 Chronicles to 2 Chronicles 36; 1 Kings 1; 2 Kings 25); King Solomon's school of leadership (1 Chronicles 28–29; 2 Chronicles 1–9); the prophethood of true and false prophets, etc. are written in the Bible for our admonition.

The Bible captures leadership in every sphere of human existence: in politics and governance, communities and nations, religions and belief systems, and family life. The Bible exposes the strength and weaknesses of men in leadership as well as their wickedness. The Bible is very explicit about the successes and failures of leaders at a different time in history without setting aside the divine requirements for true and God's kind of leadership.

There is no such book in the world as Bible. Every deed of men, whether good or bad, were never concealed; they were written for us to learn from. The book reveals the kinds of people who had led at one time or the other, the set of people that will always emerge to lead in a type of generation, the position of God on leadership, and who qualifies to lead others.

The leadership criteria by God are fixed from the foundation of the world; it does not change with what is trending in the world system. Therefore, there can never be any adequate research document that can captures types of leaders that will always emerge from one generation to another other than the Bible.

The Bible describes every generation that had emerged and others that will evolve. The Bible says: *"Wherein unto shall l likened this generation?"* (Matthew 11:16)

Deuteronomy 32:5 describes perverse and wicked generation; a stubborn and rebellious generation is identified in Psalm 78:8; Proverbs 30:13 identifies generation with lofty eyes; Proverbs 30:14 identifies generation whose teeth are like swords; and generation that are pure in their own eyes is mentioned in Proverbs 30:12.

Generations of vipers, adulterous generation, wicked and adulterous generation that seek for signs, faithless and perverse generation, and generation that seek for signs are revealed in Matthew 12:24, 11:39, 16:4, 17:17, and 8:12 respectively.

This time and season in the world are a generation of more people whose love for God is waxing cold, worldliness has overtaken the heart of men, God's truth is daily compromised, people are following broad ways to get to the top, and people are only interested in God for provision of bread only. The generation we are in is the one where younger ones are learning wickedness, perversion, and all forms of ungodliness from which are the undoing of the older ones.

God is continually grieved by generation whose measure of performance is worldly gazette and not what the Word of God says. God is angry with the generation who loves wages of unrighteousness and perverse the truth. God cannot overlook men who provide leadership that is not derived from godliness, truth, mercy, justice, service to humanity, selflessness, holiness, righteousness, self-control, purity, transparency, accountability, and a regenerative life in Jesus Christ.

The leaders of these generations say there is peace where there is no peace; they say there is a way when they have sunk in the deep; they cajole men and promise what is not in their capacity to deliver; they are running after shadows and complicate the troubles in the lives of the governed.

These leaders are in position for their self-satisfaction; they are full of deceits and manipulations. They call darkness, light; and light, darkness. And they are subtle and rob their people of God's giving commonwealth.

The Failure of Leadership

What has failed or is failing in leading men is caused by the undoing of men saddled with responsibilities of leadership.

Every generation fails because its leaders fail God.

The success of leadership has been reduced only to meeting the aspiration of the lead, when in actual fact, leadership success begins with whether leaders who are in charge are chosen by God, how God sees them, and the name God called them.

Psalm 69:35, *"For God will save Zion, and will build the cities of Judah: that they may dwell there, and have it in possession,"* and Psalm 127:1, *"Except the LORD build the house, they labour in vain that build it: except the LORD keep the city, the watchman waketh but in vain,"* presume God as one that has capacity to build our world through men.

It is not in the power of any man to lead others, and neither is it in a man's ability to provide leadership that is required to build a people and their commonwealth—only God does.

When men who are saddled with responsibility to build the lives of others do so without God, their entire efforts amount to nothing.

I have raised him up in righteousness, and I will direct all his ways: he shall build my city, and he shall let go my captives, not for price nor reward, saith the LORD of hosts. (Isaiah 45:13)

And they that shall be of thee shall build the old waste places: thou shalt raise up the foundations of many generations; and thou shalt be called, The repairer of the breach, The restorer of paths to dwell in. (Isaiah 58:12)

Until a leader is chosen by God, he stands the risk of working alone, and eventually have all his celebrated successes eroded.

A leader might provide basic amenities for his people and yet still fail God's leadership test.

There are many successful bad leaders across nations of the world whose achievements are still being celebrated up till today but are rejected by God because what they have accomplished are not with a perfect heart. Such leaders align themselves to the natural laws of leadership but fail to please God in critical areas of their lives.

The failure in leadership might have negative short-term and long-term effects in the lives of the led which sometimes might not be witnessed in the time of the leaders. The Bible reveals shortcomings in the lives of many leaders which are lessons for us.

The leadership performance is better gauged spiritually, lest we ignore divine requirements for leadership and refer to a criminal as a good leader because he has been able to provide basic amenities alone.

The second book of Chronicles says, *"Amaziah was twenty and five years old when he began to reign and he reigned twenty and nine years in Jerusalem, And his mother's name was Jehoaddan of Jerusalem. And he did that which was right in the sight of the Lord but not with a perfect heart."* (2 Chronicles 25:1–2)

Every time men approach leadership with a natural mindset, there bounds to be failure and when leaders fail, the destiny of the lead is susceptible to jeopardy.

Adam in Leadership

Adam was given a leadership role in the garden of Eden but failed because of three major reasons.

1. He ignored God's given instruction and accepted his wife's counsel at the most critical time in their lives just because of their desire to be like God.
2. He was not ready to take full responsibility for his failure and rather engaged in "blame game."
3. He allowed their predicament to becloud his sense of responsibility to instill godly character in Cain.

The failure of Adam in leadership brought everlasting devastation to his children (Cain and Abel) and the entire race (Genesis 3:6–12, 4:1–11).

Eli in Leadership

Eli was the priest of the Lord armed with divine knowledge to lead the nation of Israel in the way of the Lord. Over a long period of time, Eli was never found wanting in God's service but was careless to first lead his household in the ways of God. What were responsible for Eli's leadership failures are:

1. Eli qualified his children for divine position when they were not morally and spiritually fit.

2. Eli indirectly refused to rebuke his children when they were going wrong.
3. Eli was enjoying the respect that came with his exalted position in the land of Israel; therefore, he was in the habit of covering up the defects in the lives of his children.
4. Eli's wife also must have been enjoying all the reverences that people of Israel accorded their family but failed to at least hold home front for her husband when he was always at God's service.
5. Though Eli was old when his children were ordained as priests to be judges over Israelites, it shows that when the children were infants, Eli and his wife failed in leading them in the way to go (1 Samuel 2:11–17, 22–24).

Samuel in Leadership

One would have expected the sons of Prophet Samuel also to be above board by living rightly, but unfortunately, when they assumed position of leadership before the demise of their father, they turned aside and perverted judgments (1 Sam 8:1–3).

The question is, Who was at fault between Samuel and his children?

1. Samuel's leadership over his household lacked the same grip with which he ruled over Israel.
2. Samuel was aware of the reasons God dealt with Eli's family, but he did not learn from it.
3. It seems that Samuel hardly had time for his family; he was too busy with God's works without realizing that God's works begins with his family.

Rehoboam, the Son of Solomon in Leadership

1. Rehoboam's leadership embraced autocratic and dictatorial approach including divide and rule tactics.

2. Rehoboam protected his position by asking people to do evil against the Lord; he cares only for his merchandise despite against God and the people.

3. Rehoboam appointed least and unqualified men into exalted places that strictly required the upright and the just. All he desired was to have men loyal to him in power and who can do his bidding irrespective of its negative consequences.

4. This King Rehoboam was a de facto king who was in charge of everything. Even as the chief priest against the dictations of Mosaic Law, he made everyone who worked with him to enter into unholy oath with him (1 Kings 12:6–17).

Older Prophet in Leadership

The story of an old prophet versus a younger prophet in the Bible also reflect a type of leadership; because of old prophet's superior position, he misled the younger prophet so that he can be seen as the one who cut the short and who was in control, the old prophet loved to put other prophets under him through deployment of charismatic witchcraft. (1 Kings 13:18–24).

Moses in Leadership

Prophet Moses's style of leadership was a phenomenon but unfortunately, Moses's anger denied him of Promised Land despite all his labor over the children of Israel; Moses had shortcoming in his character management.

Despite that, Moses was chosen by God as the leader over Israel, yet he defaulted in one area of God's expectations for leadership; how then will a leader, who is not chosen by God, be able to meet the requirements of leadership not to talk of pleasing God? (Exodus 20:9–12).

They angered him also at the waters of strife,
so that it went ill with Moses for their sake: Because

they provoked his spirit, so that he spake unadvisedly
with his lips. (Psalm 106:32–33)

King Saul in Leadership

King Saul's style of leadership was flagrant disobedience to constituted higher authority, jealousy, and deceit. King Saul ended his
life abruptly without honor of a king, while he left Israel impoverished and with a great loss.

It is not all traditional beliefs that are against God, but very
many of them are mere human philosophies that originate from their
perceptions and the devil (the initiator of such ways of life), which
in most cases run contrary to the ways of God. And if God's ways are
not our ways, then there will always be a difference between man's
views on leadership and that of God. (1 Samuel 15:1–35).

One of the acceptable grounds of providing leadership in our
time all over the world is alignment with international charter on
human right that upholds rights of men to living in some ways that
are either in compliance or in gross disobedience to God's. Apart
from basic rights to living, which are ordained by God, people's rights
are so defined as if men created themselves; men are now at liberty
to decide what is good for them such as homosexualism, lesbianism,
gay priesthood, regulated pornography, regulated harlotry, regulated
intake of hard drugs, and many rights that have been embraced by
world system of leadership against God's defined ways for human
living.

Few notable nations in the world have officially assented to
"world liberal order" which allows men to choose how to live without
strict adherence to the requirements for living by God. Some world
leaders who have raised the bar of ungodliness and unholiness are
being celebrated across many nations. To worsen the case, some of
these leaders claim to belong to *the Church of Christ.*

In Nigeria, there was a legend who was not only immortalized
but he has been called a superior leader and a prophet. He lived a
life as a musician, addicted to drugs and marijuana and promiscuity.
Every year he is being remembered for a legacy that had destroyed

many lives, and even till now, destinies of millions of men are in jeopardy because of the embracement of what the leader in question lived for. What a shame and misrepresentation of definition of true leadership!

> The more men neglect the acts of God in leadership, the more complicated, perverted and difficult life becomes for the living among them.

What then shall we say? Does it mean angels are the only beings that can make it to God's choice of leaders? No! Are there any qualified men in any generation to meet the demand of godly leadership? Yes!

Though God rules in the affairs of men, He has prepared men as leaders for every generation. Every generation fails because its leaders fail God.

> Every generation fails because its leaders fail God.

While many leaders fail in leadership, God has never failed. Isaiah 65:22 emphasizes God's leadership deliverables to His people: *"... They shall not build, and another inhabits; they shall not plant, and another eats: for as the days of a tree are the days of my people, and mine elect shall long enjoy the work of their hands."* There are many nations sitting on God-endowed resources and yet are impoverished. Of course, that can never be the fault of God but their leaders.

God's Criteria for Leadership

God does not have different requirements
for evolvement of leaders in different nations, and
among people of diverse languages and tribes.
He has one standard for leadership irrespective
of people's culture, tradition, and belief system.

There will always be need for leadership at spiritual levels, political levels, economic levels, social levels, parental levels, business levels, moral levels, etc.

What is incontrovertible is that *people deserve the kind of leaders that lead them* because it is their choice, directly or indirectly. God is not a man whose choices for leadership fail; God always records success in His entire endeavor—nothing prevails against His choice of leaders, and when His choices are confronted with wild challenges, their reliance and source of inspiration for victory is God.

Therefore, the strength of leadership is in its source. What constitutes a leader's authority and power is equivalent to his leadership strength and capabilities.

> The strength of leadership is in its source.
> What constitute a leader's authority and power is
> equivalent to his leadership strength and abilities.

> *The counsel of the Lord standeth for ever, the
> thoughts of his heart to all generations. Blessed is
> the nation whose God is the Lord; and the people*

34

*whom he hath chosen for his own inheritance. The
LORD looketh from heaven; he beholdeth all the sons
of men. From the place of his habitation he looketh
upon all the inhabitants of the earth. He fashioneth
their hearts alike; he considereth all their works.
There is no king saved by the multitude of an host:
a mighty man is not delivered by much strength.
An horse is a vain thing for safety: neither shall he
deliver any by his great strength.* (Psalm 33:11–17)

*"For my thoughts are not your thoughts, nei-
ther are your ways my ways," saith the LORD. "For
as the heavens are higher than the earth, so are my
ways higher than your ways, and my thoughts than
your thoughts. For as the rain cometh down, and the
snow from heaven, and returneth not thither, but
watereth the earth, and maketh it bring forth and
bud, that it may give seed to the sower, and bread
to the eater: So shall my word be that goeth forth
out of my mouth: it shall not return unto me void,
but it shall accomplish that which I please, and it
shall prosper in the thing whereto I sent it. For ye
shall go out with joy, and be led forth with peace:
the mountains and the hills shall break forth before
you into singing, and all the trees of the field shall
clap their hands. Instead of the thorn shall come up
the fir tree, and instead of the brier shall come up
the myrtle tree: and it shall be to the LORD for a
name, for an everlasting sign that shall not be cut
off."* (Isaiah 55:8–13)

Naturally, the thoughts of men seem right to them, and this
informs their decision of whom they prefer to lead them. Most times,
men place high premium on what is on sight than what is hidden,
and because of this grievous weakness and shortcoming in men, peo-

ple who aspire to become leaders put on a picture of what is visible to the eyes and what appeals to their emotion.

Because these evolving leaders have mastered the craft of behaving, appearing, and presenting themselves in the way people want them, they ended up being selected, appointed, nominated, supported, and elected. These terrible leaders smartly capitalize on poverty that has made their subjects to lose control of their mind and made them to embrace life and living without choice.

Where there is no godly leadership or leaders, there will be indecorum, disorderliness, confusion, and all forms of perversion.

I have been hearing men saying, "After all, the governor or any other public/private leader has done something. Therefore, he is better than the former one even though he steals money."

Some people also say, "Why are you dabbling into his/her private or unofficial life? After all he/she is performing his/her official duties."

> The crucible of true leadership at all levels of human endeavors is not primarily on whether he is accepted by men and whether the leader has been able to meet certain needs but is to please God first.

The book of Revelation 4:11 says: "*God created all things including men for His pleasure.*"

> A leader maybe acceptable to men and yet not approved by God.

> Until a man is first led by God, he will never be able to lead men in the ways of God.

> When mere men are in leadership, then the leadership thrust will be shifted from God. Man only has leadership responsibility placed on him. Only God has leadership thrust in Him.

Therefore, except if a man is being led by God, all his efforts as a leader, which might seem to be productive or yield some applaudable results, will not at long last satisfy the needs of the lead.

> Except if a man is being led by God, all his efforts as a leader, which might seem to be productive or yield some applaudable results, will not at long last satisfy the needs of the lead.

The book of Jeremiah 17:5–8 says, *"Thus said the Lord; cursed be the man that trusteth in man, and maketh flesh his arm, whose heart depart from the Lord. For he shall be like the heath in the desert, and shall not see when good cometh; but shall inhabit the parched places in the wilderness in a salt land and not inhabited. Blessed is the man that trusteth in the Lord, and whose hope the Lord is."*

Therefore, searching out criteria for leadership in the Bible (the greatest book on leadership) will help nations, individuals, organizations, and every manned institution to make the choice of God their choice.

> When the choice of God is men's choice as leaders, there will always be direct access to divine wisdom to excel at all fronts in leadership positions.

The Bible is explicit on men and women who were appointed as leaders by God in their generations, and some of these leaders still failed in one area or the other. If that were the case, what then will become of leaders that are appointed /selected/elected by men?

Therefore, there are critical requirements by God for leadership, and that is the reason He is never in a haste to raise leaders for His people. The unprepared and untested men can never make it to the list of God's choice of leaders.

> The unprepared and untested men can never make it to the list of God's choice of leaders.

The physique of Eliab and his popularity were not in any way considered by God to anoint him as king in place of King Saul for the nation of Israel. His gifts of prophecies in Korah and Dathan did not qualify them to be in leadership with Moses, and God did not find in Absalom godly qualities for leadership as the next king after David, his father.

Though, Esau was the firstborn but lacked capacity to assume position of first-born leader for the household of Isaac. There were still many Israelis at the then-ruined Jerusalem but were never considered by God to lead in the rebuilding-Jerusalem project, but their brothers who had been taken into slavery from childhood were.

There were many agile and battle-ready men in the time of Prophetess Deborah but lacked what God needed at that time for leadership, except Deborah. The trained combatants in the army of Israel were put aside by God to provide leadership against Goliath, but He chose David, a seventeen-year-old lad.

God faulted the preparation of 31,700 soldiers and settled for 300 battalion squad as army of Gideon against a joint force of their enemies.

Jehoash was seven years old when the responsibility of leadership was placed on him, where elderly men old enough to have given birth to his father were alive. Despite the foothold of Pharaoh as the king of Egypt in the time of Joseph, God was able to entrust leadership to a prisoner called Joseph who possibly knew little or nothing about economy theories and governance.

God takes His time—no matter the urgency of the needs of men—to search, prepare, and announce His choice of leaders for the people. God is never democratic about His choice; He never places untested men without resilient godly character to lead His people. God raises leaders as shepherd shepherding his flock.

God raises leaders as shepherd shepherding his flock.

Thou leddest thy people like a flock by the hand of Moses and Aaron. (Psalm 77:20)

But made his own people to go forth like sheep, and guided them in the wilderness like a flock. (Psalm 78:52)

He shall feed his flock like a shepherd: he shall gather the lambs with his arm, and carry them in his bosom, and shall gently lead those that are with young. (Isaiah 40:11)

"When God's choice is men's choice as leaders, there will be direct access to divine wisdom and all the required capacity for optimal and satisfying leadership."

The counsel of the LORD standeth forever, the thoughts of his heart to all generations. Blessed is the nation whose God is the LORD; and the people whom he hath chosen for his own inheritance. (Psalm 33:11–12)

"For my thoughts are not your thoughts, neither are your ways my ways," saith the LORD. "For as the heavens are higher than the earth, so are my ways higher than your ways, and my thoughts than your thoughts." (Isaiah 55:8–9)

Ho, every one that thirsteth, come ye to the waters, and he that hath no money; come ye, buy, and eat; yea, come, buy wine and milk without money and without price. Wherefore do ye spend money for that which is not bread? and your labour for that which satisfieth not? hearken diligently unto me, and eat ye that which is good, and let your soul delight itself in fatness. Incline your ear, and come unto me: hear, and your soul shall live; and I will make an everlasting covenant with you, even the sure mercies of David.

> *Behold, I have given him for a witness to*
> *the people, a leader and commander to the people.*
> *Behold, thou shalt call a nation that thou know-*
> *est not, and nations that knew not thee shall run*
> *unto thee because of the LORD thy God, and for*
> *the Holy One of Israel; for he hath glorified thee.*
> (Isaiah 55:1–5)

Examining the first five verses of the book of Prophet Isaiah 55:1–5, critical to leadership among men are:

- *All men created by God cannot solve their problems alone.*
- *The problems of men are diverse and are either physical or spiritual, and either material or immaterial, or both.*
- *Meeting all the needs of men is by covenant, which is premised on God's mercies and grace and only on divine provisions and supply.*
- *God knows the right person(s) that can be used to provide leadership required to meet such needs.*

The emphasis is on verses 4 and 5: *"Behold, I have given him for a witness to the people, a leader and a commander to the people. Behold thou shall call a nation that knoweth not, and nations that knew not shall run unto thee because the LORD thy God and for the Holy one of Israel; for he had glorified thee."*

The choice of God as leaders among men has the key to unlock every situation to favor men. This choice of men by God are endued with divine power, wisdom, knowledge, insight, revelation, and understanding to turn wilderness to habitation, unlock potentials, and make the best use of every circumstance to put a smile in the face of men.

This choice of leaders by God have access to God's heart to resolve complexities and create a great conducive environment for all men without compromising the requirement of holiness, truth, righteousness, and the leadership principles of Jesus Christ in whom the fullness of all things that pertain to Godhead dwells bodily.

Godly Criteria for Leadership and His Choice of Leaders

The first criterion for the choice of leaders by God is having a place in *Him* and being known by *Him*. The acceptance of Jesus Christ as the Lord over one's life and as one's personal savior and that of the whole world is the foremost step to be taking in becoming a choice of leader in God's hand.

In other words, the person(s) that will be qualified by God to lead others must be born-again; he will be someone who had acknowledged his/her sins, inadequacies, shortcomings, wrongdoings, and weaknesses and confess them with a genuine intention to forsake them, repent of them, and ask for forgiveness which is received by the cleansing power in the blood of Jesus that was shed on the cross of Calvary.

The Bible says, "For all have sinned and come short of the glory of the Lord." Except our nature is under the control of higher and godly authority, which we receive after being genuinely born again; our case will be like blinds leading the blinds.

> *Let them alone: they be blind leaders of the blind. And if the blind lead the blind, both shall fall into the ditch.* (Matthew 15:14)

What the Bible says about the nature of man is that it is inimical to the lives of others because it is sinful, corrupt, wicked, selfish, disobedient, filthy, deceitful, full of lies, and with high potency to increase the sorrow and unsatisfaction of people he is leading or may lead.

> *The heart is deceitful above all things, and desperately wicked: who can know it?* (Jeremiah 17:9)

> *And GOD saw that the wickedness of man was great in the earth, and that every imagination of*

the thoughts of his heart was only evil continually.
(Genesis 6:5)

> *And the* LORD *smelled a sweet savour; and the*
> LORD *said in his heart, "I will not again curse the*
> *ground any more for man's sake; for the imagination*
> *of man's heart is evil from his youth; neither will I*
> *again smite any more everything living, as I have*
> *done.* (Genesis 8:21)

However inadequate and unqualified a man is, when he has been to Jesus Christ the savior, he gets transformed to become like Jesus and, therefore, has his nature under the influence and control of the Holy Spirit.

> *Therefore, if any man be in Christ, he is a*
> *new creature: old things are passed away; behold all*
> *things are become new.* (2 Corinthians 5:17)

> *Having abolished in his flesh the enmity, even*
> *the law of commandments contained in ordinances;*
> *for to make in himself of twain one new man, so*
> *making peace.* (Ephesians 2:15)

> *And, having made peace through the blood of*
> *his cross, by him to reconcile all things unto himself;*
> *by him, I say, whether they be things in earth, or*
> *things in heaven. And you, that were sometime alien-*
> *ated and enemies in your mind by wicked works,*
> *yet now hath he reconciled in the body of his flesh*
> *through death, to present you holy and unblameable*
> *and unreproveable in his sight.* (Colossian 1:20–22)

God cannot behold iniquities even though He forgives iniq-uities—His nature is pure, holy, and righteous; and He operates through earthen vessels that are clean and fill with His holy nature. If

God rules in the affairs of men, it means He provides right leadership through His Holy vessels to meet the needs of men.

> *And God sent me before you to preserve you a posterity in the earth, and to save your lives by a great deliverance.* (Genesis 45:7)

> *The hands of Zerubbabel have laid the foundation of this house; his hands shall also finish it; and thou shalt know that the LORD of hosts hath sent me unto you.* (Zechariah 4:9)

> *This matter is by decree of the watchers and the demand by the word of the holy ones, with the intent that living may know that the Most High ruleth in the kingdom of men, giveth it to whomsoever He will, and setteth up over it the baseth of men.* (Daniel 4:17)

> *And by a prophet the LORD brought Israel out of Egypt, and by a prophet was he preserved.* (Hosea 12:10)

Jesus Christ is God that came in human form who demonstrated how to raise leaders, how to deploy leaders, and what it takes to provide leadership. Jesus's divine purpose is to save the world from her depravity that has permeated leadership at all levels of human life. Jesus achieved this by offering Himself to die gruesomely for the sins of all men.

Because sins hinder a man to lead right or to gain insight into the mind of God in providing purposeful and profitable leadership, Jesus paid the ultimate price of death to reconcile men who acknowledge, confess, forsake, and repent of their sins to God.

> *For God so loved the world, that he gave his only begotten Son, that whosoever believeth in him*

should not perish, but have everlasting life. (John 3:16)

Who hath believed our report? And to whom is the arm of the LORD *revealed? For he shall grow up before him as a tender plant, and as a root out of a dry ground: he hath no form nor comeliness; and when we shall see him, there is no beauty that we should desire him. He is despised and rejected of men; a man of sorrows, and acquainted with grief: and we hid as it were our faces from him; he was despised, and we esteemed him not. Surely he hath borne our griefs, and carried our sorrows: yet we did esteem him stricken, smitten of God, and afflicted. But he was wounded for our transgressions, he was bruised for our iniquities: the chastisement of our peace was upon him; and with his stripes we are healed.*

"All we like sheep have gone astray; we have turned everyone to his own way; and the LORD *hath laid on him the iniquity of us all. He was oppressed, and he was afflicted, yet he opened not his mouth: he is brought as a lamb to the slaughter, and as a sheep before her shearers is dumb, so he openeth not his mouth. He was taken from prison and from judgment: and who shall declare his generation? for he was cut off out of the land of the living: for the transgression of my people was he stricken. And he made his grave with the wicked, and with the rich in his death; because he had done no violence, neither was any deceit in his mouth. Yet it pleased the* LORD *to bruise him; he hath put him to grief: when thou shalt make his soul an offering for sin, he shall see his seed, he shall prolong his days, and the pleasure of the* LORD *shall prosper in his hand.*

"He shall see of the travail of his soul, and shall be satisfied: by his knowledge shall my righteous ser-

*vant justify many; for he shall bear their iniqui-
ties. Therefore, will I divide him a portion with the
great, and he shall divide the spoil with the strong;
because he hath poured out his soul unto death: and
he was numbered with the transgressors; and he bare
the sin of many, and made intercession for the transgressors."* (Isaiah 53:1–end)

> *Having predestinated us unto the adoption of
> children by Jesus Christ to himself, according to the
> good pleasure of his will, To the praise of the glory of
> his grace, wherein he hath made us accepted in the
> beloved.*
>
> *In whom we have redemption through his
> blood, the forgiveness of sins, according to the riches
> of his grace; Wherein he hath abounded toward us
> in all wisdom and prudence.* (Eph 1:5–8)

Therefore, there is no religion or any other man that had been able to reconcile men back to God other than Jesus Christ. Jesus is the wisdom of God by which all things were made—He is the word of God and was with God before all things were made; He is the reason for life and the reason we live, and by Him, all men's hope is rekindled.

The Bible emphasizes on Jesus that *"In Him was life; and the life was the light of men. And the light shineth in darkness; and the darkness comprehended it not. There was a man sent from God, whose name was John. The same came for a witness, to bear witness of the Light, that all men through him might believe. He was not that Light, but was sent to bear witness of that Light. That was the true Light, which lighteth every man that cometh into the world"* (John 1:5–9).

> *And there shall come forth a rod out of the
> stem of Jesse, and a Branch shall grow out of his
> roots: And the spirit of the LORD shall rest upon him,
> the spirit of wisdom and understanding, the spirit*

of counsel and might, the spirit of knowledge and of the fear of the LORD; *And shall make him of quick understanding in the fear of the* LORD: *and he shall not judge after the sight of his eyes, neither reprove after the hearing of his ears:*

But with righteousness shall he judge the poor, and reprove with equity for the meek of the earth: and he shall smite the earth with the rod of his mouth, and with the breath of his lips shall he slay the wicked. And righteousness shall be the girdle of his loins, and faithfulness the girdle of his reins. (Isaiah 11:1–5)

That the God of our Lord Jesus Christ, the Father of glory, may give unto you the spirit of wisdom and revelation in the knowledge of him: The eyes of your understanding being enlightened; that ye may know what is the hope of his calling, and what the riches of the glory of his inheritance in the saints.

And what is the exceeding greatness of his power to us-ward who believe, according to the working of his mighty power, Which he wrought in Christ, when he raised him from the dead, and set him at his own right hand in the heavenly places,

Far above all principality, and power, and might, and dominion, and every name that is named, not only in this world, but also in that which is to come: And hath put all things under his feet, and gave him to be the head over all things to the church, Which is his body, the fullness of him that filleth all in all." (Ephesians 1:17–23)

For by him were all things created, that are in heaven, and that are in earth, visible and invisible, whether they be thrones, or dominions, or principal-

ities, or powers: all things were created by him, and for him: And he is before all things, and by him all things consist.

And he is the head of the body, the church: who is the beginning, the firstborn from the dead; that in all things he might have the preeminence. For it pleased the Father that in him should all fullness dwells. (Colossians 1:16–19)

The Bible emphasizes that it pleased the Father that the fullness of all things dwells in Jesus Christ.

Give ear, O Shepherd of Israel, thou that leads Joseph like a flock; thou that dwellest between the cherubims, shine forth. Before Ephraim and Benjamin and Manasseh stir up thy strength, and come and save us.

Turn us again, O God, and cause thy face to shine; and we shall be saved. O LORD God of hosts, how long wilt thou be angry against the prayer of thy people?

Thou feedest them with the bread of tears; and givest them tears to drink in great measure. Thou makest us a strife unto our neighbours: and our enemies laugh among themselves. Turn us again, O God of hosts, and cause thy face to shine; and we shall be saved.

Thou hast brought a vine out of Egypt: thou hast cast out the heathen, and planted it. Thou preparedst room before it, and didst cause it to take deep root, and it filled the land. The hills were covered with the shadow of it, and the boughs thereof were like the goodly cedars. She sent out her boughs unto the sea, and her branches unto the river.

Why hast thou then broken down her hedges, so that all they which pass by the way do pluck her?

The boar out of the wood doth waste it, and the wild beast of the field doth devour it. Return, we beseech thee, O God of hosts: look down from heaven, and behold, and visit this vine;

And the vineyard which thy right hand hath planted, and the branch that thou madest strong for thyself. It is burned with fire, it is cut down: they perish at the rebuke of thy countenance. Let thy hand be upon the man of thy right hand, upon the son of man whom thou madest strong for thyself.

So will not we go back from thee: quicken us, and we will call upon thy name. Turn us again, O LORD God of hosts, cause thy face to shine; and we shall be saved. (Psalm 80:1–end)

Psalmist arrogates all powers and authority of shepherding or leadership unto the great author of life. King David called Him the shepherd—the God of all strength, the savior and feeder of His people, the enlightener, the deliverer, and the restorer.

No man born of a woman can possess the ultimate qualities of godly leadership, except he/she has been regenerated in Christ Jesus.

I know what is carnal is not spiritual, therefore only the spiritual can understand the things that are spiritual about leadership and governance according to God's injunctions and verdicts.

The "thrust of leadership" is in the hand of Jesus for all generations. The past generations that encountered God through Jesus Christ were able to do exploits or established legacies that transcend their existence and became the pivot stands of good leadership for their children's children.

American Greatness Through Founding Fathers' Leadership

The American greatness from inception was not an outcome of mere wishes but direct effect of her founding fathers or leaders whose submission to the supremacy of God was recorded, and this informed how leaders in their time emerged. Though the greatness is still there, but there are proofs at this time that the godly requirements for leadership have been watered down.

Biblical truth and God's unchanging positions on who a leader of people should be was the instruments of rebirth for personal development and service to their nation.

> Every deviation from God's principles in choosing leaders leads to unending frustration of a people, a family, a community, and a nation.

> *My people are destroyed for lack of knowledge: because thou hast rejected knowledge, I will also reject thee, that thou shalt be no priest to me: seeing thou hast forgotten the law of thy God, I will also forget thy children.* (Hosea 4:6)

> *Ah sinful nation, a people laden with iniquity, a seed of evildoers, children that are corrupters: they have forsaken the LORD, they have provoked the Holy One of Israel unto anger, they are gone away backward.* (Isaiah 1:4)

Let us run through the profiles of a few numbers of America founding fathers and their leadership inclinations.

Benjamin Rush (1745–1813) was from Pennsylvania—the surgeon general of the Continental Army—who helped found five colleges and began the Sunday school movement as well as the first American Bible society. Benjamin Rush published the first American chemistry textbook.

He was a truce breaker between John Adams and Thomas Jefferson. He was opposed to slavery and worked alongside notable Black leaders: Absalom Jones and Richard Allan during the Yellow Fever epidemic in Philadelphia in 1793. He and his wife, Julia Stockton, had thirteen children, nine of whom survived their first year.

Benjamin Rush quoted:

> The Bible, when not read in schools, is seldom read in any subsequent period of life... The Bible...should be read in our schools in preference to all other books because it contains the greatest portion of that kind of knowledge, which is calculated to produce private and public happiness.
>
> My only hope of salvation is in the infinite transcendent love of God manifested to the world by the death of His Son upon the cross. Nothing but His blood will wash away my sins. I rely exclusively upon it. Come, Lord Jesus! Come quickly!

John Jay (1745–1829) from New York served as the first chief justice of the United States. He authored Jay Treaty, which attempted to normalize trade with Britain in 1795; opposed slavery; was a governor of New York for six years; was president of the American Bible Society; and was the author of several Federalist Papers alongside Alexander Hamilton and James Madison. He and his wife, Sarah Livingston, had six children.

John Jay quoted:

> Providence has given to our people the choice of their rulers, and it is the duty, as well as the privilege and interest, of our Christian nation to select and prefer Christians for their rulers.
>
> It certainly is very desirable that a pacific disposition should prevail among all nations. [and] The most effectual way of producing it is by extending the prevalence and influence of the Gospel."

Samuel Adams (1722–1803) from Massachusetts: early revolutionary in the struggle leading up to the Declaration of Independence opposing the taxes Britain tried to enforce on the colonists and leader in the Boston Tea Party; helped to orchestrate the Continental Congress; and Jefferson called him "the man of the revolution," Governor of Massachusetts. He married Elizabeth Checkley, and they had six children—two of whom survived into adulthood. When she died in 1757, he married Elizabeth Wells. They had no children.

Samuel Adams quoted:

> The name of the Lord (says the Scripture) is a strong tower; thither the righteous flee and are safe [Proverbs 18:10]. Let us secure His favor and He will lead us through the journey of this life and at length receive us to a better.
>
> Principally, and first of all, I resign my soul to the Almighty Being who gave it, and my body I commit to the dust, relying on the merits of Jesus Christ for the pardon of my sins.

Richard Stockton (1730–1781) from New Jersey served as a lawyer who personally presented to King George III the grievances of the Stamp Act, donated land to form Princeton University and served as a trustee for twenty-six years, was captured by the British early in the conflict of 1776, and never took a pardon from the king in exchange for loyalty to the crown. He and his wife, Annis Boudinot Stockton, a notable poet, had six children.

Richard Stockton quoted:

> I...subscribe to the entire belief of the great and leading doctrines of the Christian religion, such as the being of God; the universal defection and depravity of human nature; the Divinity of the person and the completeness of the redemption purchased by the blessed Savior; the necessity of the operations of the Divine Spirit; of Divine

faith accompanied with an habitual virtuous life; and the universality of the Divine Providence.

[I] exhort and charge [my children] that the fear of God is the beginning of wisdom, that the way of life held up in the Christian system is calculated for the most complete happiness that can be enjoyed in this mortal state, [and] that all occasions of vice and immorality is injurious either immediately or consequentially—even in this life.

Noah Webster (1758–1843) from Connecticut known as the father of American scholarship and education; editor of the Federalist Papers; author of the Copyright Act; published spelling books for schools and began compiling *An American Dictionary of the English Language* in 1807, a project that took him twenty-six years to complete; helped found Amherst College; and opposed slavery. He and his wife, Rebecca Greenleaf, had eight children, five of whom survived into adulthood.

Noah Webster quoted:

The Christian religion is the most important and one of the first things in which all children under a free government ought to be instructed. No truth is more evident than that the Christian religion must be the basis of any government intended to secure the rights and privileges of a free people.

Roger Sherman (1721–1793) from Connecticut is the only person who signed all the four important founding documents from the declaration to the constitution. He served as a lawyer and the first mayor of New Haven, and introduced the cent as coinage. He and his wife, Elizabeth Hartwell, had seven children. When she died, he married Rebekah Prescott. They had eight children, six of whom survived into adulthood.

Roger Sherman quoted,

> I believe that there is one only living and true God, existing in three persons, the Father, the Son, and the Holy Ghost, the same in substance, equal in power and glory. That the Scriptures of the Old and New Testaments are a revelation from God, and a complete rule to direct us how we may glorify and enjoy Him.
>
> I believe a visible church to be a congregation of those who make a credible profession of their faith in Christ, and obedience to Him, joined by the bond of the covenant.

Charles Carroll (1737–1832) was from Maryland and was the only Roman Catholic to sign the Declaration of Independence. He helped draft the Maryland Constitution, was the first US Senator from Maryland, and established the Baltimore and Ohio Railroad in retirement. He married Molly Darnall. They had seven children, three of whom survived into adulthood.

Charles Carroll quoted,

> On the mercy of my Redeemer I rely for salvation and on His merits, not on the works I have done in obedience to His precepts.
>
> Without morals a republic cannot subsist any length of time; they therefore who are decrying the Christian religion, whose morality is so sublime and pure, [and] which denounces against the wicked eternal misery, and [which] insured to the good eternal happiness, are undermining the solid foundation of morals, the best security for the duration of free governments.

George Mason (1725–1792), who was a native of Virginia, adamantly opposed the United States Constitution, fearing its overreach.

He authored Virginia's Constitution and the Virginia Declaration of Rights which became the basis of the United States Bill of Rights. He and his wife, Anne Eilbeck, had nine children.

George Mason quoted,

> My soul I resign into the hands of my Almighty Creator, whose tender mercies are all over His works, who hateth nothing that He hath made, and to the justice and wisdom of whose dispensations I willingly and cheerfully submit, humbly hoping from His unbounded mercy and benevolence, through the merits of my blessed Savior, a remission of my sins.
>
> As much as I value a union of all the states, I would not admit the southern states into the union, unless they agreed to the discontinuance of this disgraceful [slave] trade, because it would bring weakness and not strength to the union.

Francis Hopkinson (1737–1791) from Pennsylvania designed the first official American Flag, played the harpsichord and was a poet, composed several songs and hymns and is considered America's first composer, served as a church director and choir leader, and served as a judge of the United States District Court. He and his wife, Ann Borden, had five children.

Francis Hopkinson quoted,

> Have mercy therefore on us, LORD. And all our hearts incline, with diligence and care to keep those righteous laws of thine.
>
> Blessed is he, who fears the LORD. And does His laws obey, great his seed shall be on Earth. His race shall not decay. Crowned with wealth, his house shall be to mercy still inclined; though in trouble, he shall shine, the blessing of mankind.

Patrick Henry (1736–1799) from Virginia worked as a criminal attorney and was known for his brilliant oratory skills, feared the constitution's overreach and helped spirit along the adoption of the Bill of Rights, served as the first governor of Virginia (and also the sixth), and he was fearful of both the spread of atheism and deism toward the end of his life. He and his wife, Sarah Shelton, had six children. After her death, he married Dorothea Dandridge, and they had eleven children.

Patrick Henry quoted,

> It cannot be emphasized too strongly or too often that this great nation was founded not by religionists, but by Christians; not on religions, but on the gospel of Jesus Christ. For that reason alone, people of other faiths have been afforded freedom of worship here.
>
> This book [The Bible] is worth all the books that ever were printed, and it has been my misfortune that I never found time to read it with the proper attention and feeling till lately. I trust in the mercy of heaven that it is not too late.

Many more founding fathers, like George Washington who helped establish a parish of Anglican church; John Adams who seems steeped in faith enough to say, "I have examined all religions, and the result is that the Bible is the best book in the world"; Alexander Hamilton who said, "I have a tender reliance on the mercy of the Almighty, through the merits of the Lord Jesus Christ. I am a sinner. I look to Him for mercy; pray for me"; and others relied absolutely on God for leadership.

Zach Kincaid wrote that "No matter where was turned to in the days of the founding fathers in America, there were Christians who helped secure a Republic that stands as 'one Nation under God, indivisible, with liberty and justice for all.' America's founding fathers were not leaders loosed with their faith and principles. They held tightly to who was making them, namely salvation through Jesus Christ alone because they knew, without any shadow of turning, that it was their only hope for glory and, more temporary, the only hope for America."

> *Jesus is the mystery behind crucible and mastery of leadership; no schools of thoughts in leadership can be lined-up or compared with His wisdom. No wonder the Scriptures says: "By me kings reign, and princes decree justice."* (Proverbs 8:15)

"Where men rule by their own strength without Jesus who is the wisdom and power of God" (1 Corinthians 1:24), there shall abound utter failure of leadership; and where anything termed worthwhile is achieved by men in their own strength, such accomplishments do not endure.

Many world leaders have their names engraved in history because of their positive impacts in the lives of their people, but such impacts get eroded, fizzled out, and will become history if the proceeds of leadership do not originate from men who have being to Jesus and have Him indwelling them.

Colossians 2:3 says, *"…In whom are hid all the treasures of wisdom and knowledge,"* and Colossians 1:19 says, *"…For it pleased the Father that in him should all fullness dwell."*

Jesus holds the key and mantle of leadership.

There is a huge difference between what acquired knowledge can deliver and what inspired wisdom can make happen. Let us examine few scriptures on what divine wisdom can deliver in leadership.

> *And I have filled him with the spirit of God, in wisdom, and in understanding, and in knowledge, and in all manner of workmanship.* (Exodus 31:3)

> *And I, behold, I have given with him Aholiab, the son of Ahisamach, of the tribe of Dan: and in the hearts of all that are wise hearted I have put wisdom, that they may make all that I have commanded thee.* (Exodus 31:6)

And Joshua the son of Nun was full of the spirit of wisdom; for Moses had laid his hands upon him: and the children of Israel hearkened unto him, and did as the LORD commanded Moses. (Deuteronomy 34:9)

And all Israel heard of the judgment which the king had judged; and they feared the king: for they saw that the wisdom of God was in him, to do judgment. (1 Kings 3:28)

And God gave Solomon wisdom and understanding exceeding much, and largeness of heart, even as the sand that is on the sea shore. And Solomon's wisdom excelled the wisdom of all the children of the east country, and all the wisdom of Egypt. (1 Kings 4:29–30)

And there came of all people to hear the wisdom of Solomon, from all kings of the earth, which had heard of his wisdom. (1 Kings 4:34)

And the LORD gave Solomon wisdom, as he promised him: and there was peace between Hiram and Solomon; and they two made a league together. (1 Kings 5:12)

There is a huge difference between what acquired knowledge can deliver and what inspired wisdom can make happen.

The thrust of leadership on Bezaleel, Aholiab, Joshua, and Solomon in the Bible texts above prove that those men lacked the requisite capacity to make happen what their leadership responsibilities demand; it is by divine wisdom they were able to do exploits as leaders.

Though one can be schooled in leadership and continually develop capacity to meet the demands of the followers, the lead may even be like or greater than his leader but will operate within the measure of his leader's belief system and capacity.

> The accomplishments, the language, the
> thought, the how, and the intention of leadership
> are encapsulated in the belief system of a leader.

Therefore, very crucial also in leadership is the lifestyle of the leader. Every leader is a product of another leader; no leader emerges from the air.

Whether someone is born with leadership traits or learn or develop the skills, you are a product of leadership provided by someone or some people at one time or the other.

No matter how skillful, intelligent, resourceful, and good leadership inclined a person is, his or her limitations and shortcomings at a time will count against his leadership.

It is only in Jesus; imperfection of a leader can be perfected—shortcomings and inadequacies can be removed or transformed.

God's Choice of Leaders

God is never in a hurry to herald anyone
into leadership position. Hophni and Phineas
were called the priests of the Lord by men, but
God called them sons of Belia.

T he world systems allow coercion, violence, and cover up to
dominate leadership space to the extent that the less or not
qualified individuals arrogate power and authority to themselves at
the expense of the wishes and demands of the lead.

Men who have no leaders over them, or who have deliberately
not yielded to any leadership or who are not accountable to God
and men, are in position of leadership in our world; we are at a more
perilous time than ever before where a few groups of people hijack
leadership and force themselves on others.

This worldly pattern of leadership is destroying the essence of
humanity and wrecking more havocs than ever imagined. Every time
men choose a leader for themselves against the desire of God, chaos,
trouble, discomfort, agony, wickedness, evil, retrogression, regret,
and sorrow rend the space of leadership. People who are the objects
of leadership become subjects of leadership.

The best of all men cannot withstand the
choice of God. The attainments of the best of
men are very little or negligible compared to the
fit attained by God's choice of leaders.

Though the best of men for leadership may be beneficial to the people, it is never to be compared to the exploits of the choice of God.

Men choose by sight; that is, by what they can see—what is visible and is presented to them which may not necessarily be the truth.

God never chose by sight; He knows everyone before conception, when he was born, what he is doing unknown to others, and what may turn out to be in future. Nothing is hidden from God about any mortal man, for He alone created them.

Only listening, learning, active, team-bounded and bonded, humble, innovative, discipline, impartial, influencing, process compliance, and target driven men find favor with God to lead in any capacity.

Some of the choices of God as leaders over His people include: The choice of David:

> …But the LORD said unto Samuel, "Look not on his countenance, or on the height of his stature; because I have refused him." For the LORD seeth not as man seeth; for man looketh on the outward appearance, but the LORD looketh on the heart. Then Jesse called Abinadab, and made him pass before Samuel. And he said, "Neither hath the LORD chosen this." Then Jesse made Shammah to pass by. And he said, "Neither hath the LORD chosen this."
>
> Again, Jesse made seven of his sons to pass before Samuel. And Samuel said unto Jesse, "The LORD hath not chosen these." And Samuel said unto Jesse, "Are here all thy children?" And he said, "There remaineth yet the youngest, and, behold, he keepeth the sheep." And Samuel said unto Jesse, "Send and fetch him: for we will not sit down till he come hither."
>
> And he sent, and brought him in. Now he was ruddy, and withal of a beautiful countenance, and goodly to look to. And the LORD said, "Arise, anoint

him: for this is he." Then Samuel took the horn of oil and anointed him in the midst of his brethren: and the Spirit of the LORD came upon David from that day forward. So Samuel rose up, and went to Ramah... (1 Samuel 16:7–13)

The choice of Jeremiah:

> *...Then the word of the LORD came unto me, saying, "Before I formed thee in the belly I knew thee; and before thou camest forth out of the womb I sanctified thee, and I ordained thee a prophet unto the nations." Then said, "Ah, Lord GOD! Behold, I cannot speak: for I am a child."*
>
> *But the LORD said unto me, "Say not, I am a child: for thou shalt go to all that I shall send thee, and whatsoever I command thee thou shalt speak. Be not afraid of their faces: for I am with thee to deliver thee, saith the LORD... "* (Jeremiah 1:4–8)

The choice of Jehoash:

> *...Seven years old was Jehoash when he began to reign...* (2 Kings 11:21)

> *In the seventh year of Jehu Jehoash began to reign; and forty years reigned he in Jerusalem. And his mother's name was Zibiah of Beersheba. And Jehoash did that which was right in the sight of the LORD all his days wherein Jehoiada the priest instructed him...* (2 Kings 12:1–2)

The choice of Esther:

> *...And he brought up Hadassah, that is, Esther, his uncle's daughter: for she had neither*

*father nor mother, and the maid was fair and beau-
tiful; whom Mordecai, when her father and mother
were dead, took for his own daughter.*

*So it came to pass, when the king's command-
ment and his decree was heard, and when many
maidens were gathered together unto Shushan the
palace, to the custody of Hegai, that Esther was
brought also unto the king's house, to the custody of
Hegai, keeper of the women.*

*...And the king loved Esther above all the
women, and she obtained grace and favour in his
sight more than all the virgins; so that he set the
royal crown upon her head, and made her queen
instead of Vashti...* (Esther 2:7–8, 17)

The choice of Naman:

*Now Naaman, captain of the host of the king
of Syria, was a great man with his master, and hon-
ourable, because by him the LORD had given deliverance unto Syria: he was also a mighty man in
valour, but he was a leper.* (2 Kings 5:1)

The choice of Deborah:

*...And the children of Israel cried unto the LORD:
for he had nine hundred chariots of iron; and twenty
years he mightily oppressed the children of Israel.
And Deborah, a prophetess, the wife of Lapidoth, she
judged Israel at that time...* (Judges 4:3–4)

The choice of Moses:

*Now therefore, behold, the cry of the children
of Israel is come unto me: and I have also seen the
oppression wherewith the Egyptians oppress them.*

Come now therefore, and I will send thee unto Pharaoh, that thou mayest bring forth my people the children of Israel out of Egypt. And Moses said unto God, Who am I, that I should go unto Pharaoh, and that I should bring forth the children of Israel out of Egypt? (Exodus 3: 9–11)

The choice of Gideon:

And there came an angel of the LORD, and sat under an oak which was in Ophrah, that pertained unto Joash the Abiezrite: and his son Gideon threshed wheat by the winepress, to hide it from the Midianites. And the angel of the LORD appeared unto him, and said unto him, The LORD is with thee, thou mighty man of valour.

*And Gideon said unto him, "Oh my Lord, if the LORD be with us, why then is all this befallen us? And where be all his miracles which our fathers told us of, saying, 'Did not the LORD bring us up from Egypt?' But now the LORD hath forsaken us, and delivered us into the hands of the Midianites."
And the LORD looked upon him, and said, "Go in this thy might, and thou shalt save Israel from the hand of the Midianites: have not I sent thee?" And he said unto him, "Oh my Lord, wherewith shall I save Israel? Behold, my family is poor in Manasseh, and I am the least in my father's house."* (Judges 6:11–15)

The choice of Saul called Paul:

And there was a certain disciple at Damascus, named Ananias; and to him said the Lord in a vision, Ananias. And he said, "Behold, I am here, Lord." And the Lord said unto him, "Arise, and go into the street which is called Straight, and enquire in the house of Judas for one called Saul, of Tarsus: for, behold, he prayeth, And hath seen in a vision a man named Ananias coming in, and putting his hand on him, that he might receive his sight."

Then Ananias answered, "Lord, I have heard by many of this man, how much evil he hath done to thy saints at Jerusalem: And here he hath authority from the chief priests to bind all that call on thy name." But the Lord said unto him, "Go thy way: for he is a chosen vessel unto me, to bear my name before the Gentiles, and kings, and the children of Israel:" (Acts 9:10–15)

Because God knows the aftermath of any event or occurrence ahead of time, He raises men to meet its demands. Though God is concerned with every occurrence, He works daily to guarantee an expected end or a great future for the works of His hands.

Therefore, God's choice of leaders is tied to His purpose and not what men may desire except the desires of men are aligned to His.

God's choice of leaders is tied to His purpose.

God chooses people who cherish peace among men in leadership.

These people see God in everyone, try everything possible to be at peace with others, and put high premium on human lives than their ambitions; they are not coercive leaders but ones who have won the hearts of their followers, and they are very calm in the face of utter challenges.

Though they are humans, they have learned how to put their bodies under; they demonstrate an act of self-control in every situation. They are true shepherds who will not abandon a sheep to perish.

Contrary to God's demand on leadership, the world system embraces leaders that are violent—men who bring the world down to remain in power and subject their subjects to servitude.

Across the world, the majority of the celebrated leaders are infamous: they live for themselves; they are violent, deceitful, selfish, destructive, and manipulative.

> *Follow peace with all men, and holiness, without which no man shall see the Lord.* (Hebrews 12:14)

> *Finally, brethren, farewell. Be perfect, be of good comfort, be of one mind, live in peace; and the God of love and peace shall be with you.* (2 Corinthians 13:11)

> *But the fruit of the Spirit is love, joy, peace, long-suffering, gentleness, goodness, faith.* (Galatians 5:22)

> *Let us therefore follow after the things which make for peace, and things wherewith one may edify another.* (Romans 14:19)

God chooses men that are dutiful and service-minded.

Lazy and self-serving men are burdens to leadership; they become albatross to the lead. These leaders do not serve men but are being served. To them, a leadership position is an exalted position of authority and not of service. The crop of such leaders places responsibility of leadership on their subjects, but quick to take glory for successes.

> *The hand of the diligent shall bear rule: but the slothful shall be under tribute.* (Proverbs 12:24)

> *Seest thou a man diligent in his business? he shall stand before kings; he shall not stand before mean men.* (Proverbs 22:29)

God heralds to leadership men who have or exercise control over their lives at every situation.

Everyone who first sees himself always in all matters personalizes issues in leadership. It becomes difficult for such men to exercise control in leading others. Their weaknesses and shortcomings are easily identified and often become the cause of great distress to the people they are leading.

> *He that is slow to anger is better than the mighty; and he that ruleth his spirit than he that taketh a city.* (Proverbs 16:32)

> *He that hath no rule over his own spirit is like a city that is broken down, and without walls.* (Proverbs 25:28)

God raises leaders that live for others even at their own expense.

> *And Moses said unto Aaron, "Take a censer, and put fire therein from off the altar, and put on incense, and go quickly unto the congregation, and make an atonement for them: for there is wrath gone out from the LORD; the plague is begun." And Aaron took as Moses commanded, and ran into the midst of the congregation; and, behold, the plague was begun among the people: and he put on incense, and made an atonement for the people. And he stood between the dead and the living; and the plague was stayed."* (Numbers 16:46–46)

> *I am the good shepherd: the good shepherd giveth his life for the sheep.* (John 10:11)

The choice of God for leadership is people who have learned how to lean on God for wisdom and direction at all times.

> *And he said unto him, "If thy presence go not with me, carry us not up hence. For wherein shall it be*

known here that I and thy people have found grace in thy sight? Is it not in that thou goest with us? So shall we be separated, I and thy people, from all the people that are upon the face of the earth." And the LORD said unto Moses, "I will do this thing also that thou hast spoken: for thou hast found grace in my sight, and I know thee by name." (Exodus 33:15–17)

...Give me now wisdom and knowledge, that I may go out and come in before this people: for who can judge this thy people, that is so great? (2 Chronicles 1:10)

Wisdom is the principal thing; therefore get wisdom: and with all thy getting get understanding. (Proverbs 4:7)

Only the upright and just people make it to God's choice of leaders.

He that worketh deceit shall not dwell within my house: he that telleth lies shall not tarry in my sigh. (Psalm 101:7)

The Spirit of the LORD spake by me, and his word was in my tongue. The God of Israel said, the Rock of Israel spake to me, He that ruleth over men must be just, ruling in the fear of God." (2 Samuel 23:2–3)

While it is not really the skills and experience that makes a man to succeed in godly leadership position but those who have demonstrated accomplishments in little things are giving consideration by God for leadership.

We have many leaders across the board, especially at these times, who have never demonstrated success in any of their personal businesses, including their homes but who are leading people and establishments in bigger responsibilities.

The examples of men called to leadership by God below show how important success in what a person finds doing is to God before being saddled with mantle of leadership.

Gideon was found threshing. (Judges 6:11)

Elisa was a successful farmer. (1 Kings 19:19)

Moses was a successful herdsman. (Exodus 3:1)

All the disciples of Jesus were not left out, and among them were fishermen, lawyers, tax managers, etc.

Only people who first lived by example are choosing by God to lead others.

Arm-chaired men are not God's choice for leadership except the people who are epistles of their messages, dictates, and who live to meet the demands of their leadership.

The former treatise have I made, O Theophilus, of all that Jesus began both to do and teach. (Acts 1:1)

We proclaim to you the one who existed from the beginning, whom we have heard and seen. We saw him with our own eyes and touched him with our own hands. He is the Word of life. (1 John 1: 1)

The only letter of recommendation we need is you yourselves. Your lives are a letter written in our hearts; everyone can read it and recognize our good work among you. (2 Corinthians 3:2)

Here I am. Witness against me before the LORD *and before His anointed: Whose ox have I*

*taken, or whose donkey have I taken, or whom have
I cheated? Whom have I oppressed, or from whose
hand have I received any bribe with which to blind
my eyes? I will restore it to you.* (1 Samuel 12:3)

*And you should imitate me, just as I imitate
Christ.* (1 Corinthians 11:1)

*For I have known him, in order that he may
command his children and his household after him,
that they keep the way of the LORD, to do righteousness and justice, that the LORD may bring to Abraham
what He has spoken to him.* (Genesis 18:19)

Because leadership is spiritual in the sense that it has to do with
management of human beings whose nature is more spiritual than
physical, God considers uniqueness of individual persons as leaders
by putting a square peg in a square hole.

*And He Himself gave some to be apostles, some
prophets, some evangelists, and some pastors and
teachers...* (Ephesians 4:11)

The choice of a man who is demonstrating selflessness and lives
for impact is critical to God.

*So the king asked me, "Why are you looking so
sad? You don't look sick to me. You must be deeply
troubled." Then I was terrified, but I replied, "Long
live the king! How can I not be sad? For the city
where my ancestors are buried is in ruins, and the
gates have been destroyed by fire." The king asked,
"Well, how can I help you?"
With a prayer to the God of heaven, I replied,
"If it please the king, and if you are pleased with
me, your servant, send me to Judah to rebuild the*

city where my ancestors are buried." (Nehemiah 2:2–5)

"Go and gather together all the Jews of Susa and fast for me. Do not eat or drink for three days, night or day. My maids and I will do the same. And then, though it is against the law, I will go in to see the king. If I must die, I must die." So Mordecai went away and did everything as Esther had ordered him. (Esther 4:16–17)

Those who have not been doing well in managing human relationships at all levels and are not willing to learn the act of doing so are not in God's list of leaders because the fulcrum of leadership is capacity and capability to manage human relationship.

Pursue peace with all people, and holiness, without which no one will see the Lord. (Hebrews 12:14)

But then David's conscience began bothering him because he had cut Saul's robe. He said to his men, "The LORD forbid that I should do this to my lord the king. I shouldn't attack the LORD's anointed one, for the LORD himself has chosen him." (1 Samuel 24:5–6)

The fulcrum of leadership is the capacity and capability to manage human relationships.

Only men with godly intentions and intents are His choice as leaders of others.

Intention is a fundamental principle of leadership and a framework for the creation of ultimate reality. It's the building plans for reality. Before a leader comes up with a plan, he must have gotten an intention; the thought of what he wants to see happen, or what his ultimate goal is.

When it was day, the Jews formed a conspiracy and bound themselves under an oath, saying that they would neither eat nor drink until they had killed Paul. There were more than forty who formed this plot. They came to the chief priests and the elders and said, "We have bound ourselves under a solemn oath to taste nothing until we have killed Paul." (Acts 23:12–22)

Then the Lord saw that the wickedness of man was great on the earth, and that every intent of the thoughts of his heart was only evil continually. (Genesis 6:5)

For the word of God is living and active and sharper than any two-edged sword, and piercing as far as the division of soul and spirit, of both joints and marrow, and able to judge the thoughts and intentions of the heart. (Hebrews 4:12 NASB1995)

Man sees your actions, but God sees your motives. (pinterest.com)

God values deeds according to their intentions. For it is said, "The Lord grant unto you according to your heart" (Psalm 19:5)

Therefore, whoever wants to do something but can't is considered as having done it by God, who sees the intentions of our hearts. This applies to both good and evil deeds alike. (Marcus Eremita)

The furtherance of leadership and what becomes of it is a function of the intentions of a leader.

The seed of leadership grows on the soil of intentions, whether good or bad.

God gives leadership position to any man based on his capability. God will not give a highly demanding responsibility to any leader who has not demonstrated excellence, or is making progress in little or commensurate responsibility.

> *If you are faithful in little things, you will be faithful in large ones. But if you are dishonest in little things, you won't be honest with greater responsibilities.* (Luke 16:10)

When God places a demand on a leader and he is faithful, except the leader continues to serve His purpose without drawing back in the face of tribulations; God may not hesitate to replace him.

> *And a voice said, "What are you doing here, Elijah?" He replied again, "I have zealously served the Lord God Almighty. But the people of Israel have broken their covenant with you, torn down your altars, and killed every one of your prophets. I am the only one left, and now they are trying to kill me, too."*
>
> *Then the Lord told him, "Go back the same way you came, and travel to the wilderness of Damascus. When you arrive there, anoint Hazael to be king of Aram. Then anoint Jehu grandson of Nimshi to be king of Israel, and anoint Elisha son of Shaphat from the town of Abel-meholah to replace you as my prophet. Anyone who escapes from Hazael will be killed by Jehu, and those who escape Jehu will be killed by Elisha! Yet I will preserve 7,000 others in Israel who have never bowed down to Baal or kissed him!"* (1 Kings 19:13b–18)

God searches for leaders that can reproduce themselves. Every man whose leadership's gospel and practice do not arouse the birth of other formidable leaders will be replaced by God even while on duties.

Everything God created produces, increases, and multiplies after its own kind. Both plants and humans are wired by God to reproduce their kinds. Good and bad leaders reproduce their kinds. God expects harvest of godly leaders from the source of any good leader He has raised for the people.

> *Then God said," Let the earth bring forth… that yields seed and the fruit tree that yields fruit according to its kind, whose seed is in itself, on the earth." It was so.* (Genesis 1: 11)

> *Now be fruitful and multiply, and repopulate the earth.* (Genesis 9:7)

> *Therefore, go and make disciples of all the nations, baptizing them in the name of the Father and the Son and the Holy Spirit.* (Matthew 28:19)

God is not a respecter of anyone. From one generation to another, His purpose and accomplishment is put on the shoulders of His choice of leaders. When leaders fail their constituents, God is never stranded; He raises other leaders to accomplish His purpose.

> *Then the word of the Lord came to Samuel: "I regret that I have made Saul king, because he has turned away from me and has not carried out my instructions." Samuel was angry, and he cried out to the Lord all that night… For rebellion is like the sin of divination, and arrogance like the evil of idolatry. Because you have rejected the word of the Lord, he has rejected you as king." (1 Samuel 15:10–11, 23)*

> *Now the Lord said to Samuel, "You have mourned long enough for Saul. I have rejected him as king of Israel, so fill your flask with olive oil and go to Bethlehem. Find a man named Jesse who lives there, for I have selected one of his sons to be my king."* (1 Samuel 16:1)

Because a leader is the brand image of the people being led, God is never carried away by physique and what are attractive to sight to appoint a leader.

> *When they arrived, Samuel took one look at Eliab and thought, "Surely this is the Lord's anointed!" But the Lord said to Samuel, "Don't judge by his appearance or height, for I have rejected him." The Lord doesn't see things the way you see them. People judge by outward appearance, but the Lord looks at the heart.* (1 Samuel 16:6–7)

The spirit of servanthood dominates the heart of God's chosen leader; he lives for others, and he is unrepentantly living by the golden rule that says: whatever you will not want anyone do unto you, don't do unto others.

> *But among you it will be different. Whoever wants to be a leader among you must be your servant.* (Matthew 20:26)

> *I also told everyone living outside the walls to stay in Jerusalem. That way, they and their servants could help with guard duty at night and work during the day. During this time, none of us—not I, nor my relatives, nor my servants, nor the guards who were with me—ever took off our clothes. We carried our weapons with us at all times, even when we went for water.* (Nehemiah 4:22–23)

Mordecai in Leadership

Mordecai was Jewish slave like others who was one of the servants of King Ahasuerus.

He sleeps by the king's gate.

Life was not comfortable for him yet refused to forsake the Lord in his afflictions.

He raised Esther, an orphan and a slave to become the queen of Ahasuerus—a king of over 127 provinces (states).

He inspired the Israelites in the land of slavery to serve the Lord.

He defiled not himself with the largesse of corruption in the kingdom of Ahasuerus.

He vehemently refused to bow down for and revere Haman, a vile person who feared not the Lord of Israel.

The Foolishness of God Revealed

> Everything that does not profit God first before it profits men will spell doom for human race.

The greatest enemy of man is himself; his doing is what undoes him. Exercising his will most times puts him in precarious situations and subjects his life to unwholesome burden, and when he is very confident of his decisions or defends his actions and reactions, regrets and failures characterize his world.

The greatest threat to humanity is when men think they are sufficient in themselves to make the world a better place. Leading men must be to the profit of God first before it can be profitable to men; therefore, only God is enough for mankind—only the wisdom of God is required to manage all the resources, therein including men.

The ways of God, His wisdom, and the leadership He provides are at variance with the desires of men except in few cases their desires are in subjection to the will of God. If God's ways and thoughts are not men's, definitely God and man will always be doing and seeing things differently.

> *For my thoughts are not your thoughts, neither are your ways my ways, saith the* Lord. *For as the heavens are higher than the earth, so are my ways higher than your ways, and my thoughts than your thoughts.* (Isaiah 55:8–9)

How foolish is God? Why do some of His actions defile logics, rationalism, and acceptable norms? Why are some of His choices at variance with organized bodies of knowledge? Why are God's leadership criteria mostly incongruent to the proven research by men? Why is God's way difference from that of men?

> *Because the foolishness of God is wiser than men; and the weakness of God is stronger than men.* (1 Corinthians 1:25)

> *But the natural man receiveth not the things of the Spirit of God: for they are foolishness unto him: neither can he know them, because they are spiritually discerned.* (1 Corinthians 2:14)

> *For the wisdom of this world is foolishness with God. For it is written, He taketh the wise in their own craftiness.* (1 Corinthians 3:19)

Why do many considerable factors for choosing leaders among men seem to be inconsequential to God or less considered by Him?

Why will God set aside human leadership philosophy and settle for what does not align with democratic principles and earthly system of governance?

What will Jehoash bring to leadership at the age of seven over a nation that parades the elderly, the experienced, the princes and the clan leaders, the mayors, the wealthy people, the prophets, and the priests of God?

> *...Seven years old was Jehoash when he began to reign...* (2 Kings 11:21)

What explanation can we give to a prisoner—Joseph—without any economy degree, becoming a leader in a strange land at the most critical time in the land of Egypt? What was God thinking?

> *...And Pharaoh said unto Joseph, "See, I have set thee over all the land of Egypt." And Pharaoh took off his ring from his hand, and put it upon Joseph's hand, and arrayed him in vestures of fine linen, and put a gold chain about his neck; And he made him to ride in the second chariot which he had; and they cried before him, "Bow the knee:" And he made him ruler over all the land of Egypt. And Pharaoh said unto Joseph, "I am Pharaoh, and without thee shall no man lift up his hand or foot in all the land of Egypt..."* (Genesis 41:41–44)

Why did God approve less than 0.1% of the army of 32,000 men to go with Gideon to war against consortium of army generals and soldiers of enemy nations?

Even though Gideon was a valiant man, yet there was no record of him to have fought in that capacity before then; so why his choice, by God, to lead a historical battle against the enemies of Israel?

> *...Now therefore go to proclaim in the ears of the people, saying, "Whosoever is fearful and afraid, let him return and depart early from mount Gilead." And there returned of the people twenty and two thousand; and there remained ten thousand...*
>
> *And the LORD said unto Gideon, "By the three hundred men that lapped will I save you, and deliver the Midianites into thine hand: and let all the other people go every man unto his place..."* (Judges 7:3, 7; 1 Samuel 14:6)

What proven knowledge of combat did Deborah, a prophet, have to lead a nation of Israel in war against their enemy? Why Deborah, and not men of war in all the tribes of Israel?

> *...And Barak said unto her, "If thou wilt go with me, then I will go: but if thou wilt not go with*

me, then I will not go." And she said, "I will surely go with thee: notwithstanding the journey that thou takest shall not be for thine honour; for the LORD shall sell Sisera into the hand of a woman." And Deborah arose, and went with Barak to Kedesh... (Judges 4:8–9)

What was of interest to God in David to be anointed a king over Israel when his exposed brothers who had been trained in the art of war were available?

...But the LORD said unto Samuel, "Look not on his countenance, or on the height of his stature; because I have refused him:" For the LORD seeth not as man seeth; for man looketh on the outward appearance, but the LORD looketh on the heart. Then Jesse called Abinadab, and made him pass before Samuel. And he said, "Neither hath the LORD chosen this." Then Jesse made Shammah to pass by. And he said, "Neither hath the LORD chosen this."

Again, Jesse made seven of his sons to pass before Samuel. And Samuel said unto Jesse, "The LORD hath not chosen these." And Samuel said unto Jesse, "Are here all thy children?" And he said, "There remaineth yet the youngest, and behold, he keepeth the sheep." And Samuel said unto Jesse, "Send and fetch him: for we will not sit down till he come hither."

And he sent, and brought him in. Now he was ruddy, and withal of a beautiful countenance, and goodly to look to. And the LORD said, "Arise, anoint him: for this is he." Then Samuel took the horn of oil and anointed him in the midst of his brethren: and the Spirit of the LORD came upon David from that day forward. So Samuel rose up, and went to Ramah... (1 Samuel 16:7–13)

What is the relationship God considered between being a keeper of domestic animals and being in charge of men that made Him to anoint David, a seventeen-year-old boy, as the king over Judah, Samaria, and Israel?

> *...And Samuel said unto Jesse, "Are here all thy children?" And he said, "There remaineth yet the youngest, and, behold, he keepeth the sheep." And Samuel said unto Jesse, "Send and fetch him: for we will not sit down till he come hither."* (1 Samuel 16:11)

Why would God prefer the weaklings of David to war veterans in his ranks of soldiers as great men of David?

> *...David therefore departed thence, and escaped to the cave Adullam: and when his brethren and all his father's house heard it, they went down thither to him. And every one that was in distress, and every one that was in debt, and every one that was discontented, gathered themselves unto him; and he became a captain over them: and there were with him about four hundred men...* (1 Samuel 22:1–2)

Why did God go for Elisha in place of Elijah despite that he was neither a Levite nor from a lineage of a prophet but from the tribe of Issachar?

> *...So he departed thence, and found Elisha the son of Shaphat, who was plowing with twelve yoke of oxen before him, and he with the twelfth: and Elijah passed by him, and cast his mantle upon him...* (1 Kings 19:19)

Why were the first two disciples of Jesus Christ fishermen and not among the scribes, the Sanhedrin, the political juggernauts in Israel, and/or members of His family first?

> *...And Jesus, walking by the sea of Galilee, saw two brethren, Simon called Peter, and Andrew his brother, casting a net into the sea: for they were fishers. And he saith unto them, "Follow me, and I will make you fishers of men. And they straightway left their nets, and followed him..."* (Matthew 18–20)

Why did God choose David instead of Jonathan despite the later display of capacity to lead?

> *...And Jonathan smote the garrison of the Philistines that was in Geba, and the Philistines heard of it. And Saul blew the trumpet throughout all the land, saying, Let the Hebrews hear...* (1 Samuel 13:3)

> *...And Jonathan said to the young man that bare his armour, "Come, and let us go over unto the garrison of these uncircumcised: it may be that the LORD will work for us: for there is no restraint to the LORD to save by many or by few..."* (1 Samuel 14:6)

What is the rationale behind the choice of Saul who later became Paul—a man who, at a critical time the church was born, was the chief persecutor of the brethren?

> *...And I persecuted this way unto the death, binding and delivering into prisons both men and women...* (Acts 22:4)

...And I punished them oft in every synagogue, and compelled them to blaspheme; and being exceedingly mad against them, I persecuted them even unto strange cities... (Acts 26:11)

...And labour, working with our own hands: being reviled, we bless; being persecuted, we suffer it: (1 Corinthians 4:12)

...For I am the least of the apostles, that am not meet to be called an apostle, because I persecuted the church of God... (1 Corinthians 15:9)

How do we interpret a scenario where God birthed revival and heaven-conscious assemblies across the world by the hands of unlettered men?

Now when they saw the boldness of Peter and John, and perceived that they were unlearned and ignorant men, they marvelled; and they took knowledge of them, that they had been with Jesus. (Acts 4:13)

At that time Jesus answered and said, "I thank thee, O Father, Lord of heaven and earth, because thou hast hid these things from the wise and prudent, and hast revealed them unto babes." (Mark 11:25)

But God hath chosen the foolish things of the world to confound the wise; and God hath chosen the weak things of the world to confound the things which are mighty. (1 Corinthians 1:27)

Why Moses, a stammerer, and not Aaron in the first place to lead Israelites out of Egypt?

> *...And Moses said unto the LORD, "O my Lord, I am not eloquent, neither heretofore, nor since thou hast spoken unto thy servant: but I am slow of speech, and of a slow tongue..."* (Exodus 4:10)

Why did God prefer Jacob to Esau despite the former's errors?

> *...And he said, "Is not he rightly named Jacob? For he hath supplanted me these two times: he took away my birthright; and, behold, now he hath taken away my blessing." And he said, "Hast thou not reserved a blessing for me..."* (Genesis 27:36)

What was of interest to God in the life of Nehemiah, a slave and a mere cupbearer to be the chosen one to rebuild the wall of ruined Jerusalem?

> *...And I said unto the king, "If it please the king, and if thy servant have found favour in thy sight, that thou wouldest send me unto Judah, unto the city of my fathers' sepulchres, that I may build it..."* (Nehemiah 1:5)

Were there no other priests in Jerusalem of more public acceptance than an exiled priest, Ezra, to be the one to rebuild the ruined temple in Jerusalem?

> *...This Ezra went up from Babylon; and he was a ready scribe in the law of Moses, which the LORD God of Israel had given: and the king granted him all his request, according to the hand of the LORD his God upon him...* (Ezra 7:6)

Why would God prefer Solomon to his brothers who seem to have learned the scope of leadership of Israel through their father, David?

> *...And Zadok the priest took an horn of oil out of the tabernacle, and anointed Solomon. And they blew the trumpet; and all the people said, God save king Solomon...* (1 Kings 1:39)

The Bible details the unthinkable, the unbelievable, the illogical, the irrational, the abnormal, and the foolish choices of God against the reasoning and validity of men of who a leader should be. Though there may be a meeting point between the choice of God and that of men, yet it does not imply that men know what is best for them in leadership.

More than enough of the choices of men as leaders end as disaster; this choice of men has increased the complexities of humanhood and makes life unbearable for the living.

There is a leader that fits a time and season, there is a leader that is already prepared by God for a task, there is a leader tied to fulfillment of a divine purpose, and there is a leader that may never be selected or elected or appointed through democratic means but is still the choice of God.

More than enough of the choices of men as leaders end as disaster.

How to Divinely Govern Men

God rules in the affairs of men.

> *Cry aloud, spare not, lift up thy voice like a trumpet, and shew my people their transgression, and the house of Jacob their sins.*
>
> *Yet they seek me daily, and delight to know my ways, as a nation that did righteousness, and forsook not the ordinance of their God: they ask of me the ordinances of justice; they take delight in approaching to God.* (Isaiah 58:1–2)

> *And I said, "Hear, I pray you, O heads of Jacob, and ye princes of the house of Israel; Is it not for you to know judgment? Who hate the good, and love the evil; who pluck off their skin from off them, and their flesh from off their bones; Who also eat the flesh of my people, and flay their skin from off them; and they break their bones, and chop them in pieces, as for the pot, and as flesh within the caldron."* (Micah 3:1–3)

Today's world, and even before now, continually degenerate into a people who do not want God to have any say in how they live and be governed; it is indeed more pronounced at this time because of already-established world order of liberalism and many more destructive ways of life that are not only a deliberate attempt to shut God out of the affairs of men but also to reenergize humanism against the dictates and instructions of God for living.

Today's leadership across the nations of the world is evolving world order of liberalism and many more destructive ways of life that are not only a deliberate attempt to shut God out of the affairs of men but also to reenergize humanism against the dictates and instructions of God for living.

This time across the world, as the Bible says, is a perilous time.

This, know also that in the last days perilous times shall come. For men shall be lovers of their own selves, covetous, boasters, proud, blasphemers, disobedient to parents, unthankful, unholy. Without natural affection, trucebreakers, false accusers, incontinent, fierce, despisers of those that are good, Traitors, heady, high-minded, lovers of pleasures more than lovers of God; Having a form of godliness, but denying the power thereof: from such turn away. For of this sort are they which creep into houses, and lead captive silly women laden with sins, led away with divers lusts. Ever learning, and never able to come to the knowledge of the truth. (2 Timothy 3:1–7)

The Bible describes the extreme end the world is tending to in terms of deviance from the original intention of God when it says the people of the world are ever learning but are always refusing the truth, are resisting the truth, are corrupt-minded, are having itching ears, are not enduring sound doctrine, are after their own lusts, and shall be heaping to themselves teachers/leaders/followers and all categories of people that are defiling the eternal providence of God for living.

These people have forgotten that though every man is born freely, no man is free from God.

> Truly men are freely born but none is free
> from God.

All men should be told that they are the works of God's hands; He made the earth and all that are within it for the comfort of men. God alone has prerogative over the lives of men and how they should live.

The devil daily contends with God's purpose for the earth, yet the standard by which men are to be living is written and sealed by God. There is no degree of utter depravity the world is subjected to that can make God to lower His standard, especially in providing leadership for men.

> There is no degree of utter depravity the
> world is subjected to that can make God to lower
> His standard in providing leadership for men."

The Bible says, "... *This matter is by the decree of the watchers, and the demand by the word of the holy ones: to the intent that the living may know that the Most High ruleth in the kingdom of men, and giveth it to whomsoever he will, and setteth up over it the basest of men*" (Daniel 4:17).

When men heap for themselves leaders that are not approved by God, the situations of the governed get worsened, and the leadership provided them becomes a snare unto them. Therefore, only the choice of leaders by God for the people upholds the demands of divine leadership.

Every leader choosing by God holds in his/her heart the following in the affairs of men.

The business of successfully leading men is of God, and so no man should think himself/herself more than a vessel in the hand of God.

Furthermore, David the king said unto all the congregation, "Solomon my son, whom alone God hath chosen, is yet young and tender, and the work is great: for the palace is not for man, but for the LORD *God."* (1 Chronicles 29:1)

For I say, through the grace given unto me, to every man that is among you, not to think of himself more highly than he ought to think. (Romans 12:3a)

For if a man think himself to be something, when he is nothing, he deceiveth himself. (Galatians 6:3)

I am the vine; you are the branches. If you remain in me and I in you, you will bear much fruit; apart from me you can do nothing. (John 15:5)

Only God's choice of leaders makes all the difference in leadership.

...And Moses spake unto the LORD, *saying, "Let the* LORD, *the God of the spirits of all flesh, set a man over the congregation, which may go out before them, and which may go in before them, and which may lead them out, and which may bring them in; that the congregation of the* LORD *be not as sheep which have no shepherd." And the* LORD *said unto Moses, "Take thee Joshua, the son of Numbers, a man in whom is the spirit, and lay thine hand upon him."* (Numbers 27:15–18)

Except the LORD *build the house, they labour in vain that build it: except the* LORD *keep the city, the watchman waketh but in vain.* (Psalm 27:1)

All leaders that have demonstrated reliance on self-experience, ability, and knowledge, though very needful, have always been failing in leading men.

> ...*And now, O* LORD *my God, thou hast made thy servant king instead of David my father: and I am but a little child: I know not how to go out or come in.* (1 Kings 3:7)

> *The way of fools seems right to them, but the wise listen to advice.* (Proverbs 12:15)

Governing or leading with the fear of God will give no room for oppression, self-centeredness, coercion, and wickedness in leadership.

> ...*Ye shall not therefore oppress one another; but thou shalt fear thy God: for I am the* LORD *your God. Take thou no usury of him, or increase: but fear thy God; that thy brother may live with thee. Thou shalt not rule over him with rigour; but shalt fear thy God.* (Leviticus 25:17, 36, 43)

> *If ye will fear the* LORD, *and serve him, and obey his voice, and not rebel against the commandment of the* LORD, *then shall both ye and also the king that reigneth over you continue following the* LORD *your God.* (1 Samuel 12:14)

There is an open door of succeeding leadership without struggle to a leader who governs in the fear of God.

> *The secret of the* LORD *is with them that fear him; and he will shew them his covenant.* (Psalm 25:14)

A leader who fears the Lord and stands for God against every form of ungodliness in leadership lacks nothing; he/she has his/her needs met by God.

> *O fear the LORD, ye his saints: for there is no want to them that fear him.* (Psalm 34:9)

Only the leaders that fear the Lord have the backing of God in leadership.

> *…There shall no man be able to stand before you: for the LORD your God shall lay the fear of you and the dread of you upon all the land that ye shall tread upon, as he hath said unto you.* (Deuteronomy 11:25; Joshua 10:8; Psalm 25:14; 34:7, 9)

Bearing rule over men to please God demands fearlessness in order to stand for Him before them. Every bit of compromise in any guise leads to spiritual suicide and utter failure in leadership.

> *…So that we may boldly say, "The Lord is my helper, and I will not fear what man shall do unto me."* (Hebrews 13:6)

> *And the LORD said unto Joshua, "Fear them not: for I have delivered them into thine hand; there shall not a man of them stand before thee."* (Joshua 10:8)

Divine governance demands resilience, boldness, courage, and perseverance. The projects in leadership become moribund where there is a continuous display of fearfulness.

> *And when the servant of the man of God was risen early, and gone forth, behold, an host compassed the city both with horses and chariots. And his servant said unto him, "Alas, my master! how shall we do?"*

And he answered, "Fear not: for they that be with us are more than they that be with them." (2 Kings 6:15–16)

And David said to Solomon his son, "Be strong and of good courage, and do it: fear not, nor be dismayed: for the LORD God, even my God, will be with thee; he will not fail thee, nor forsake thee, until thou hast finished all the work for the service of the house of the LORD." (1 Chronicles 28:20)

Have not I commanded thee? Be strong and of a good courage; be not afraid, neither be thou dismayed: for the LORD thy God is with thee whithersoever thou goest. (Joshua 1:9)

For God hath not given us the spirit of fear; but of power, and of love, and of a sound mind. (2 Timothy 1:7)

There are many leaders who are standing for men before God, thereby compromising the sanctity of divine demands on leadership to please the mortals.

A godly leader stands for justice, equity, righteousness, and deterrence.

The king's strength also loveth judgment; thou dost establish equity, thou executest judgment and righteousness in Jacob. (Psalm 99:4)

A leader chosen by God embraces, demonstrates, and lives a life of truth and peace.

The law of truth was in his mouth, and iniquity was not found in his lips: he walked with me in peace and equity, and did turn many away from iniquity. (Malachi 2:6)

> *Hear this, I pray you, ye heads of the house of Jacob, and princes of the house of Israel, that abhor judgment, and pervert all equity. They build up Zion with blood, and Jerusalem with iniquity.*
> *The heads thereof judge for reward, and the priests thereof teach for hire, and the prophets thereof divine for money: yet will they lean upon the LORD, and say, "Is not the LORD among us? None evil can come upon us." Therefore shall Zion for your sake be plowed as a field, and Jerusalem shall become heaps, and the mountain of the house as the high places of the forest.* (Micah 3:9–11)

Humility and love is in the heart, and the lifestyle of God's choice of a leader. The more you love God, the greater your compassion toward men.

> *If thou shalt keep all these commandments to do them, which I command thee this day, to love the LORD thy God, and to walk ever in his ways; then shalt thou add three cities more for thee, beside these three:* (Deuteronomy 19:9)

> *In that I command thee this day to love the LORD thy God, to walk in his ways, and to keep his commandments and his statutes and his judgments, that thou mayest live and multiply: and the LORD thy God shall bless thee in the land whither thou goest to possess it.* (Deuteronomy 30:16)

> *But if any man love God, the same is known of him.* (1 Corinthians 8:3)

"He that hath my commandments, and keepeth them, he it is that loveth me: and he that loveth me shall be loved of my Father, and I will love him, and will manifest." (John 14:21)

It is the love of God by a leader that propels him to love the subjects he/she governs.

He saith unto him the third time, "Simon, son of Jonas, lovest thou me?" Peter was grieved because he said unto him the third time, "Lovest thou me?" And he said unto him, "Lord, thou knowest all things; thou knowest that I love thee. Jesus saith unto him, Feed my sheep." (John 21:17)

A leader who is representing God among men does so in humility and total submission to God. God only works with the humble, but a proud person is detestable to Him.

A man's pride shall bring him low: but honour shall uphold the humble in spirit. (Proverbs 29:23)

For thus saith the high and lofty One that inhabiteth eternity, whose name is Holy; "I dwell in the high and holy place, with him also that is of a contrite and humble spirit, to revive the spirit of the humble, and to revive the heart of the contrite ones." (Isaiah 57:15)

True humility is intelligent self-respect that keeps us from thinking too highly or too meanly of ourselves. It makes us mindful of the nobility God meant us to have. Yet it makes us modest by reminding us how far we have come short of what we can be. (Sockman)

It was pride that changed angels into devils. It is humility that makes men as angels. (Saint Augustine)

True humility is not an abject, groveling, self-despising spirit. It is but a right estimate of ourselves as God sees us. (Edwards)

Humility is strong, not bold. Quiet, not speechless. Sure, not arrogant. (Smith)

A leader that will follow after divine governance principles must be accustomed and adaptable to what is godly, honest, lovely, noble, pure, worthy, and excellent.

> *Finally, brothers and sisters, whatever is true, whatever is noble, whatever is right, whatever is pure, whatever is lovely, whatever is admirable—if anything is excellent or praiseworthy—think about such things.* (Philippians 4:8)

It is the lifestyle of a leader who is leading according to the dictate of God not to amass wealth unto himself but to serve for the prosperity of the people. There is a curse of God over swindlers and wicked persons in leadership.

> *The LORD will enter into judgment with the ancients of his people, and the princes thereof: for ye have eaten up the vineyard; the spoil of the poor is in your houses.* (Isaiah 3:14)

> *Woe unto them! For they have gone in the way of Cain, and ran greedily after the error of Balaam for reward, and perished in the gainsaying of Core.* (Jude 1:11)

> *Woe to them that devise iniquity, and work evil upon their beds! when the morning is light, they practise it, because it is in the power of their hand. And they covet fields, and take them by violence; and houses, and take them away: so they oppress a man and his house, even a man and his heritage. Therefore thus saith the* LORD; *"Behold, against this family do I devise an evil, from which ye shall not remove your necks; neither shall ye go haughtily: for this time is evil."* (Micah 2:1–3)

> *For the vineyard of the* LORD *of hosts is the house of Israel, and the men of Judah his pleasant plant: and he looked for judgment, but behold oppression; for righteousness, but behold a cry. Woe unto them that join house to house, that lay field to field, till there be no place, that they may be placed alone in the midst of the earth!* (Isaiah 5:7–8)

A leader in God's camp sees his position as a privilege that must not be abused because he will give account of his stewardship unto God.

> *His lord said unto him, "Well done, thou good and faithful servant: thou hast been faithful over a few things, I will make thee ruler over many things: enter thou into the joy of thy lord."* (Matthew 25:21)

To divinely govern is to influence people toward God and to inspire everyone in the right ways even in the face of secularism, liberalism, and human rights.

> *And God spake all these words, saying, "I am the* LORD *thy God, which have brought thee out of the land of Egypt, out of the house of bondage.*

Thou shalt have no other gods before me." (Genesis 20:1–3)

Leading men in godly manner demands exemplary living; it requires a leader doing a thing before asking others to do so.

The former treatise have I made, O Theophilus, of all that Jesus began both to do and teach. (Acts 1:1)

A leader who is standing before God for men governs by divine wisdom and not by force or coercion; true and godly leadership demands transforming lives rather than destroying it. The choice of God as leaders are those who make things better than they met it.

Teach me to do thy will; for thou art my God: thy spirit is good; lead me into the land of upright-ness. (Psalm 143:10)

And Joshua, the son of Nun, was full of the spirit of wisdom; for Moses had laid his hands upon him: and the children of Israel hearkened unto him, and did as the LORD commanded Moses. (Deuteronomy 34:9)

To divinely run the affairs of men successfully, a leader stands aloof: *Compromise*: to agree with what is less-than-defined standards in the face of the laws governing a place or is unacceptable to God either to please men or for personal gains.

No man can serve two masters: for either he will hate the one, and love the other; or else he will hold to the one, and despise the other. Ye cannot serve God and mammon. (Matthew 6:24)

Whenever evil wins, it is only by default: by the moral failure of those who evade the fact that

there can be no compromise on basic principles.
(Ayn Rand, *Capitalism: The Unknown Idea*)

In any compromise between good and evil,
it is only evil that can profit. In that transfusion
of blood which drains the good to feed the evil,
the compromise is the transmitting rubber tube.
(AYN RAND, *Atlas Shrugged*)

Unrighteousness: every act that is unjust, sinful, unfair, wicked,
not in accordance with right or justice, and above all, against the truth.

*Ye shall do no unrighteousness in judgment:
thou shalt not respect the person of the poor, nor
honour the person of the mighty: but in righteousness
shalt thou judge thy neighbour.* (Leviticus 19:15)

Making an open stand against all the ungodliness and unrighteousness which overspreads
our land as a flood is one of the noblest ways
of confessing Christ in the face of His enemies.
(John Wesley)

By unrighteousness man prospers, gains
what appears desirable, conquers enemies, but
perishes at the root. (Rabindranath Tagore)

God's wrath is his righteousness reacting
against unrighteousness. (J. I. Packer)

Lies: saying or doing what is against the truth, intent to deceive
or create a misleading impression.

*He that worketh deceit shall not dwell within
my house: he that telleth lies shall not tarry in my
sight.* (Psalm 101:7)

The getting of treasures by a lying tongue is a vanity tossed to and fro of them that seek death. The robbery of the wicked shall destroy them; because they refuse to do judgment." (Proverbs 21:6–7)

Above all, don't lie to yourself. The man who lies to himself and listens to his own lie comes to a point that he cannot distinguish the truth within him or around him, and so loses all respect for himself and for others. And having no respect, he ceases to love. (Fyodor Dostoevsky)

Things come apart so easily when they have been held together with lies. (Dorothy Allison)

Every violation of truth is not only a sort of suicide in the liar but is a stab at the health of human society. (Ralph Waldo Emerson)

False words are not only evil in themselves but they infect the soul with evil. (Plato)

We tell lies when we are afraid…afraid of what we don't know, afraid of what others will think, afraid of what will be found out about us. But every time we tell a lie, the thing that we fear grows stronger. (Tad Williams)

Personal gains: what are beneficial to self at the expense of others.

He that loveth silver shall not be satisfied with silver; nor he that loveth abundance with increase: this is also vanity. (Ecclesiastes 5:10)

And he said unto them, "Take heed, and beware of covetousness: for a man's life consisteth not

in the abundance of the things which he possesseth."
(Luke 12:15)

You build trust with others each time you choose integrity over image, truth over convenience, or honor over personal gain. (John C. Maxwell)

To excel is to reach your own highest dream. But you must also help others, where and when you can, to reach theirs. Personal gain is empty if you do not feel you have positively touched another's life. (Barbara Walters)

If faith is lacking, it is because there is too much selfishness, too much concern for personal gain. For faith to be true, it has to be generous and loving. Love and faith go together. They complete each other. (Mother Teresa)

Our politics suffers from a shortage of people who put character and country before career and personal gain. (Cal Thomas)

Perversion: to corrupt, to misrepresent, to falsify, to deviate, and to distort the original state of things, occurrences, events, matters, etc.

Better is the poor that walketh in his integrity, than he that is perverse in his lips, and is a fool. (Proverbs 19:1)

He that hath a froward heart findeth no good: and he that hath a perverse tongue falleth into mischief. (Proverbs 17:20)

Evil has no substance of its own, but is only the defect, excess, perversion, or corruption of that which has substance. (John Henry Newman)

To reverence the impersonal creation instead of the personal God who created us is a perversion designed for escaping moral accountability to the Creator. God indicts those who worship the creation instead of its Creator (Rom 1:18–23); and warns of the corruption of morals and behavior which results. (Dave Hunt)

Injustice: to pervert justice; to call evil good and good evil.

A false balance is abomination to the LORD: but a just weight is his delight. (Proverbs 11:1)

He that justifieth the wicked, and he that condemneth the just, even they both are abomination to the LORD. (Proverbs 17:15)

Woe unto them that call evil good, and good evil; that put darkness for light, and light for darkness; that put bitter for sweet, and sweet for bitter! (Isaiah 5:20)

Thou shalt not wrest the judgment of thy poor in his cause. Keep thee far from a false matter; and the innocent and righteous slay thou not: for I will not justify the wicked. And thou shalt take no gift: for the gift blindeth the wise, and perverteth the words of the righteous. (Exodus 23:6–8)

Injustice anywhere is a threat to justice everywhere. (Martin Luther King Jr.)

In keeping silent about evil, in burying it so deep within us that no sign of it appears on the surface, we are implanting it, and it will rise up a thousand-fold in the future. When we neither punish nor reproach evildoers, we are not simply protecting their trivial old age. We are thereby ripping the foundations of justice from beneath new generations. (Aleksandr I. Solzhenitsyn, *The Gulag Archipelago*, 1918–1956)

Each time a man stands up for an ideal, or acts to improve the lot of others, or strikes out against injustice, he sends forth a tiny ripple of hope, and crossing each other from a million different centers of energy and daring those ripples build a current which can sweep down the mightiest walls of oppression and resistance. (Robert F. Kennedy)

When injustice becomes law, resistance becomes duty. (Thomas Jefferson)

Always seek justice, but love only mercy. To love justice and hate mercy is but a doorway to more injustice. (Criss Jami, *Healology*)

Whoso rewardeth evil for good, evil shall not depart from his house. (Proverbs 17:13)

Violence: an act of destruction; an intention to damage, to brutalize, to be forceful, and to threaten peace for the purpose of self-gain and power.

… Their webs shall not become garments, neither shall they cover themselves with their works: their works are works of iniquity, and the act of

violence is in their hands. Their feet run to evil, and they make haste to shed innocent blood: their thoughts are thoughts of iniquity; wasting and destruction are in their paths. The way of peace they know not; and there is no judgment in their goings: they have made them crooked paths: whosoever goeth therein shall not know peace." (Isaiah 59:6–8)

Violence is the last refuge of the incompetent. (Isaac Asimov)

As long as people use violence to combat violence, we will always have violence. (Michael Berg)

A society that presumes a norm of violence and celebrates aggression, whether in the subway, on the football field, or in the conduct of its business, cannot help making celebrities of the people who would destroy it. (Lewis H. Lapham)

When liberty comes with hands dabbled in blood, it is hard to shake hands with her. (Oscar Wilde)

Violence is an admission that one's ideas and goals cannot prevail on their own merits. (Edward Kennedy)

Violence can only be concealed by a lie, and the lie can only be maintained by violence. (Aleksandr Solzhenitsyn)

Idolatry: seeking after another God; seeking God in what He had made; and denoting the worship of deity in a visible form— whether the images to which homage is paid are symbolical representations of the true God, or of the false divinities which have been made the objects of worship in his stead.

> *Thou shalt have no other gods before me. Thou shalt not make unto thee any graven image, or any likeness of any thing that is in heaven above, or that is in the earth beneath, or that is in the water under the earth: Thou shalt not bow down thyself to them, nor serve them: for I the LORD thy God am a jealous God, visiting the iniquity of the fathers upon the children unto the third and fourth generation of them that hate me; And shewing mercy unto thousands of them that love me, and keep my commandments.* (Exodus 20:4–6)

> *I am the LORD: that is my name: and my glory will I not give to another, neither my praise to graven images.* (Isaiah 42:8)

> *Ye shall make you no idols nor graven image, neither rear you up a standing image, neither shall ye set up any image of stone in your land, to bow down unto it: for I am the LORD your God.* (Leviticus 26:1)

> There is nothing so abominable in the eyes of God and of men as idolatry, whereby men render to the creature that honor which is due only to the Creator. (Blaise Pascal)

> The essence of idolatry is the entertainment of thoughts about God that are unworthy of Him. (A. W. Tozer)

> Verily, we know not what an evil it is to indulge ourselves, and to make an idol of our will. (Samuel Rutherford)

It [idolatry] means turning a good thing into an ultimate thing. (Tim Keller)

Idolatry is in a man's own thought, not in the opinion of another. (John Selden)

To have a faith, therefore, or a trust in anything, where God hath not promised, is plain idolatry, and a worshipping of thine own imagination instead of God. (William Tyndale)

Occultism: consulting other means less than God either for protection or for other benefits; belonging to a secret society for the purpose of riches, influence, power, and fame.

And the soul that turneth after such as have familiar spirits, and after wizards, to go a whoring after them, I will even set my face against that soul, and will cut him off from among his people. (Leviticus 20:6)

Stand now with thine enchantments, and with the multitude of thy sorceries, wherein thou hast laboured from thy youth; if so be thou shalt be able to profit, if so be thou mayest prevail. Thou art wearied in the multitude of thy counsels. Let now the astrologers, the stargazers, the monthly prognosticators, stand up, and save thee from these things that shall come upon thee. (Isaiah 47:12–14)

Behold, they shall be as stubble; the fire shall burn them; they shall not deliver themselves from the power of the flame: there shall not be a coal to warm at, nor fire to sit before it. (Isaiah 47:12–14)

Self-praise: is to see oneself as the reason for any accomplishment; is to present oneself to people as the one who makes things happen; and is to demand for recognition at every place of leadership engagement. Self-praise makes a leader boast of self, and indirectly or directly fail to give honor to God. Self-praise is celebration of pride that sets a person, especially a leader, in reverse gear of success.

Whatsoever that has to do with self-gratification misleads, deceives, results in unconscious deterioration of men, relies on human confidence, retains sin in the heart of man, alienates from God, and is associated with self-righteousness.

> *For I know that in me (that is, in my flesh) dwelleth no good thing: for to will is present with me; but how to perform that which is good I find not. For the good that I would I do not: but the evil which I would not, that I do.* (Roman 7:18–19)

> *I can of mine own self do nothing: as I hear, I judge: and my judgment is just; because I seek not mine own will, but the will of the Father which hath sent me.* (John 5:30)

> *For we dare not make ourselves of the number, or compare ourselves with some that commend themselves: but they measuring themselves by themselves, and comparing themselves among themselves, are not wise.* (2 Corinthians 10:12)

> *Thus saith the Lord, "Let not the wise man glory in his wisdom, neither let the mighty man glory in his might, let not the rich man glory in his riches: But let him that glorieth glory in this, that he understandeth and knoweth me, that I am the Lord which exercise lovingkindness, judgment, and righteousness, in the earth: for in these things I delight, saith the Lord."* (Jeremiah 9:23–24)

A false balance is abomination to the LORD:
but a just weight is his delight. When pride cometh,
then cometh shame: but with the lowly is wisdom.
(Proverbs 11:2)

Foolishness: the quality of being unwise and stupid; the act of lacking common sense and good judgment; weakness of intellect; weakness of mind; the act of taking foolish decisions; etc.

A leader may not be knowledgeable in all things, but he does seek more knowledge to keep abreast of what is going on and to position himself to be able to provide leadership beyond what he had known.

Every choice of God in leadership is a man who longs and thirsts for unparalleled wisdom—he becomes daily unlearned to learn; he searches out wisdom from what has been concealed; he daily meditates and thinks through the ordeals of leadership to meet the aspiration of the lead.

This type of leader seeks the face of God and meditates in God's words; he is never satisfied with what he had known, but daily craves for more knowledge to be able to continually stand as a leader of his people.

The choice of God as leaders sees yesterday's accomplishments as past. They do not glory in their past, but look ahead for a better than yesterday's achievements. Therefore, they are studious, open to learning, and ready to set aside their positions to increase their wisdom.

This choice of leaders loves corrections, rebuke, and are very ready to give way to superior knowledge. God never set a fool in leadership position because he will not meet leadership expectations but also subject the lead to become like him; the Bible says no servant is greater than his master.

The tongue of the wise useth knowledge aright:
but the mouth of fools poureth out foolishness... A
fool despiseth his father's instruction: but he that
regardeth reproof is prudent. (Proverbs 15:2, 5)

*He that trusteth in his own heart is a fool:
but whoso walketh wisely, he shall be delivered.*
(Proverbs 28:26)

*Yea also, when he that is a fool walketh by the
way, his wisdom faileth him, and he saith to everyone that he is a fool... There is an evil which I have
seen under the sun, as an error which proceedeth
from the ruler: Folly is set in great dignity, and the
rich sit in low place.* (Ecclesiastes 10:3, 5)

*Now as Jannes and Jambres withstood Moses,
so do these also resist the truth: men of corrupt minds,
reprobate concerning the faith. But they shall proceed no further: for their folly shall be manifest unto
all men, as theirs also was.* (2 Timothy 3:8–9)

Imposition: the spirit of imposition makes a leader surround himself with loyal subordinates at the expense of quality, intellect, capability, and experience. In most cases, leaders who single-handedly choose people around them do so to conceal their weaknesses, for self-benefits, and in resistance to the truth.

A loyal subordinate may not be honest, sincere, truthful, and knowledgeable, but there is no honest subordinate who will not be loyal. The success of many leaders depends on critical factor of subordinacy.

Leaders who are giving to imposition hate wise counsel from others because it makes them look inferior. Therefore, they prefer anyone who will tell them what they want to hear.

Their business of self-multiplication and expansion thrives in having sycophants around them. This crop of leaders bears rule as emperors and lords, unquestionable beings, above the law, and one with final say.

*... That at what time ye hear the sound of the
cornet, flute, harp, sackbut, psaltery, dulcimer, and*

all kinds of musick, ye fall down and worship the golden image that Nebuchadnezzar the king hath set up: And whoso falleth not down and worship- peth shall the same hour be cast into the midst of a burning fiery furnace. (Daniel 3:5–6)

And king Rehoboam consulted with the old men that stood before Solomon his father while he yet lived, and said, "How do ye advise that I may answer this people? And they spake unto him, say- ing, If thou wilt be a servant unto this people this day, and wilt serve them, and answer them, and speak good words to them, then they will be thy ser- vants for ever."

But he forsook the counsel of the old men, which they had given him, and consulted with the young men that were grown up with him, and which stood before him: And he said unto them, "What counsel give ye that we may answer this peo- ple, who have spoken to me, saying, Make the yoke which thy father did put upon us lighter?"

And the young men that were grown up with him spake unto him, saying, "Thus shalt thou speak unto this people that spake unto thee, saying, 'Thy father made our yoke heavy, but make thou it lighter unto us'; thus shalt thou say unto them, 'My little finger shall be thicker than my father's loins. And now whereas my father did lade you with a heavy yoke, I will add to your yoke: my father hath chas- tised you with whips, but I will chastise you with scourges!'" (1 Kings 12:6–11)

Bad examples: the crop of leaders God raises give all of them- selves for the sake of God who has called them; they live by exam- ple in all their engagements, both at personal and interactive lev- els. Therefore, they lead men for God and conduct themselves in the light of God's demands. Their ultimate in leadership is to make indelible marks in the lives of their subjects to the glory of Him, who gives them the privilege.

> *For I think that God hath set forth us the apostles last, as it were appointed to death: for we are made a spectacle unto the world, and to angels, and to men. We are fools for Christ's sake, but ye are wise in Christ; we are weak, but ye are strong; ye are honourable, but we are despised.*
>
> *Even unto this present hour we both hunger, and thirst, and are naked, and are buffeted, and have no certain dwelling place; And labour, working with our own hands: being reviled, we bless; being persecuted, we suffer it: Being defamed, we intreat: we are made as the filth of the world, and are the offscouring of all things unto this day.* (1 Corinthians 4:9–13)

The Wisdom from Above

*How much better is it to get wisdom than gold!
And to get understanding rather to be chosen than
silver!* (Proverbs 16:16)

The extent of a man's intellectual capacity may speak volume on his resilience and quality of thoughts but may never suffice for the magnitude of his performance in dealing with men.

Wisdom is an intangible, unquantifiable, and limitless instrumentality of power and authority in leadership.

The greatest asset of a leader is wisdom from above; the kind of wisdom that God puts in a man to make the difference in his world.

Divine wisdom distinguishes God's choice from men of timber and caliber considered, chosen, referred, and reverenced in leadership; it is beyond the acquired wisdom of men in all their getting. It confounds the sage, the knowledgeable, the researchers, the philosophers, and all the wise men of this world.

Wisdom, though literarily defined as correct application of knowledge, is a divine gift—a heavenly deposit in man to contend for and attain mastery in leadership.

There is such a mastery a person gains in his/her profession after many years of routine engagement in a particular operation, but divine wisdom can't be acquired through career or profession; it is indeed an intangible product of God's knowledge in man that fill his/her being: his mouth, his lips, his soul, and his spirit.

While education empowers people to develop enormous capacity for growth and development, wisdom from above helps them to decipher and manage situations and to proffer solutions to very complex issues and problems around them.

> The extent of a man's intellectual capacity may speak volumes on his resilience and quality of thoughts but may never suffice for the magnitude of his performance in dealing with men.

The most complex creature God made is man; no other man has been able to tame others in the strength of who he is and what he knows except in the strength of God's wisdom.

The Bible says wisdom is a principal factor, and it is very constant; that is, every other thing depends on it. What is principal is what is first; it is what all other efforts depend on. And it is what will deliver the results of providing leadership.

> No one can succeed in managing men beyond the wisdom of God in him. It is not acquired knowledge that generates wisdom to lead people. It is God's invaluable gift of wisdom that makes the difference.

Though knowledge influences thought processes, it does not deliver good, very good, and excellent outcomes in dealing with human complexities. Nothing can be built without wisdom. (Proverbs 24:3).

> It is not acquired knowledge that generates wisdom to lead people. It is God's invaluable gift of wisdom that makes the difference.

From the time of Abraham till this day, men of great exploits (the ones that gladdens the heart of God and directly impacting men for God) are decked with uncommon wisdom to do what is infeasible, what is beyond human knowledge, and what has not crossed the thoughts of men.

Wisdom is a mystery and a revelation of God at work through men. Only those who are endowed with it lead men successfully irrespective of the enormity of challenges.

But we speak the wisdom of God in a mystery, even the hidden wisdom, which God ordained before the world unto our glory: (1 Corinthians 2:7)

Which things also we speak, not in the words which man's wisdom teacheth, but which the Holy Ghost teacheth; comparing spiritual things with spiritual. (1 Corinthians 2:13)

When Solomon ascended the throne as the king over Israel, he was very young in age and without any record of being in any position of providing leadership. Yes, he must have been understudied by his father, David, in the running of the affairs of Israel, yet there was no information on any experience he had gotten.

Though the Bible did not specify how old was Solomon when he became a king, the historical facts suggest his age to be twenty to twenty-five, and Solomon also called himself a little child in 1 Kings 3:7.

At a tender age, Solomon had responsibilities of providing leadership for all the Israelites despite Israel being alienated among other nations and surrounded by sworn enemies.

Solomon was to reign over the captains of thousands and of hundreds; the judges; all the governors in Israel; the chief of the fathers; all the clans of the twelve tribes (that is, the twelve nations);

etc. The Bible describes the population of Judah and Israel as the sand which is by the sea in multitude, and that Solomon reigned over all kingdoms from the river unto the land of the Philistines and unto the border of Egypt (1 Kings 4:20–21).

Solomon became the king over Israel at the time of great uprising, conflict, and jostling for power in the household of David; it was indeed a dreadful time to have Joab as the commander in charge of Israelite army.

How Solomon navigated the challenges of that time successfully to the extent that the Bible says, there was not even a war between Israel, and other nations resulted from the deposit of wisdom from above.

> *For he had dominion over all the region on this side the river, from Tiphsah even to Azzah, over all the kings on this side the river: and he had peace on all sides round about him. And Judah and Israel dwelt safely, every man under his vine and under his fig tree, from Dan even to Beersheba, all the days of Solomon.* (1 Kings 4:24–25)

This was Solomon's prayers to God when he was enthroned as king over Israel:

> *And Solomon went up thither to the brasen altar before the LORD, which was at the tabernacle of the congregation, and offered a thousand burnt offerings upon it. In that night did God appear unto Solomon, and said unto him, "Ask what I shall give thee. And Solomon said unto God, Thou hast shewed great mercy unto David my father, and hast made me to reign in his stead.*
> *"Now, O LORD God, let thy promise unto David my father be established: for thou hast made me king over a people like the dust of the earth in multitude. Give me now wisdom and*

> *knowledge, that I may go out and come in before this people: for who can judge this thy people, that is so great?"*
>
> *And God said to Solomon, "Because this was in thine heart, and thou hast not asked riches, wealth, or honour, nor the life of thine enemies, neither yet hast asked long life; but hast asked wisdom and knowledge for thyself, that thou mayest judge my people, over whom I have made thee king:*
>
> *"Wisdom and knowledge is granted unto thee; and I will give thee riches, and wealth, and honour, such as none of the kings have had that have been before thee, neither shall there any after thee have the like."* (2 Chronicles 1:6–12)

The wisdom of God in Solomon was more than his fame; he was wiser than any other king that had ever lived before him and during his reign.

> *Howbeit I believed not the words, until I came, and mine eyes had seen it: and, behold, the half was not told me: thy wisdom and prosperity exceedeth the fame which I heard.* (1 Kings 10:7)
>
> *Wisdom and knowledge is granted unto thee; and I will give thee riches, and wealth, and honour, such as none of the kings have had that have been before thee, neither shall there any after thee have the like." ...And Solomon's wisdom excelled the wisdom of all the children of the east country, and all the wisdom of Egypt.* (1 Kings 4:12, 30)

On account of Solomon's wisdom, many other influential personalities, like Queen of Sheba, came to learn at his feet; they were amazed at the level of his deep knowledge and how successful he was as a king over a nation of people like the dust of the earth in multitude.

> *And all the earth sought to Solomon, to hear his wisdom, which God had put in his heart.* (1 Kings 10:24)

> *And when the queen of Sheba had seen all Solomon's wisdom, and the house that he had built, And the meat of his table, and the sitting of his servants, and the attendance of his ministers, and their apparel, and his cupbearers, and his ascent by which he went up unto the house of the LORD; there was no more spirit in her.*
> *And she said to the king, "It was a true report that I heard in mine own land of thy acts and of thy wisdom. Howbeit I believed not the words, until I came, and mine eyes had seen it: and, behold, the half was not told me: thy wisdom and prosperity exceedeth the fame which I heard. Happy are thy men, happy are these thy servants, which stand continually before thee, and that hear thy wisdom."* (1 Kings 10:5–8)

The wisdom of Solomon made him exceedingly rich; many unsolicited gifts were brought to him from far places, and he enjoyed full cooperation of all the surrounding governments and became the first of all the kings such that everyone wanted to identify with him.

> *"So king Solomon exceeded all the kings of the earth for riches and for wisdom. And all the earth sought to Solomon, to hear his wisdom, which God had put in his heart. And they brought every man his present, vessels of silver, and vessels of gold, and garments, and armour, and spices, horses, and mules, a rate year by year.*
> *And Solomon gathered together chariots and horsemen: and he had a thousand and four hundred chariots, and twelve thousand horsemen, whom he bestowed in the cities for chariots, and with the king at Jerusalem.*

And the king made silver to be in Jerusalem as stones, and cedars made he to be as the sycomore trees that are in the vale, for abundance.

And Solomon had horses brought out of Egypt, and linen yarn: the king's merchants received the linen yarn at a price. And a chariot came up and went out of Egypt for six hundred shekels of silver, and an horse for an hundred and fifty: and so for all the kings of the Hittites, and for the kings of Syria, did they bring them out by their means." 1Ki 10:23-29

The betterment of divine wisdom than any other criteria for leadership is revealed in the book of life as follows:

Wisdom is a gift from God.

> *And the LORD gave Solomon wisdom, as he promised him: and there was peace between Hiram and Solomon; and they two made a league together.* (1 Kings 5:12)

> *Only the LORD give thee wisdom and understanding, and give thee charge concerning Israel, that thou mayest keep the law of the LORD thy God.* (1 Chronicles 22:12)

> *With the ancient is wisdom; and in length of days understanding. With him is wisdom and strength, he hath counsel and understanding.* (Job 12:12–13)

> *If any of you lack wisdom, let him ask of God, that giveth to all men liberally, and upbraideth not; and it shall be given him.* (James 1:5)

Wisdom refers to as the Spirit of God.

> *And I have filled him with the spirit of God, in wisdom, and in understanding, and in knowledge, and in all manner of workmanship.* (Exodus 31:3)

Wisdom is a deposit in the heart or spirit of man, and not in his head.

> *And Moses called Bezaleel and Aholiab, and every wise hearted man, in whose heart the LORD had put wisdom, even everyone whose heart stirred him up to come unto the work to do it.* (Exodus 36:2)

There is such thing as "spirit of wisdom" which makes wisdom an intangible, unquantifiable, and limitless instrumentality of power and authority in leadership.

> *And Joshua the son of Nun was full of the spirit of wisdom; for Moses had laid his hands upon him: and the children of Israel hearkened unto him, and did as the LORD commanded Moses.* (Deuteronomy 34:9)

Wisdom is termed "spirit of excellence or distinction." What distinctively differentiates one leader from another is divine wisdom inherent in them.

> *Then this Daniel was preferred above the presidents and princes, because an excellent spirit was in him; and the king thought to set him over the whole realm.* (Daniel 6:3)

Man gains access to divine wisdom by fearing God.

> *The fear of the LORD is the beginning of wisdom: a good understanding have all they that do his commandments: his praise endureth for ever.* (Psalm 111:10)

> *The fear of the LORD is the beginning of wisdom: and the knowledge of the holy is understanding.* (Proverbs 9:10)

The righteous and the upright in heart have access to God's wisdom.

> *He layeth up sound wisdom for the righ-*
> *teous: he is a buckler to them that walk uprightly.*
> (Proverbs 2:7)

Leadership yields good inheritance and profit by wisdom.

> *Wisdom is good with an inheritance: and by it*
> *there is profit to them that see the sun.* (Ecclesiastes 7:1)

Wisdom is better than strength, and wisdom strengthens.

> *Then," said I, "wisdom is better than strength.*
> (Ecclesiastes 9:16a)

> *Wisdom strengtheneth the wise more than*
> *ten mighty men which are in the city.* (Ecclesiastes
> 7:19)

Divine wisdom is a defense, and its presence reenergizes, resuscitates, and empowers a leader at the time of need.

> *For wisdom is a defence, and money is a*
> *defence: but the excellency of knowledge is, that wis-*
> *dom giveth life to them that have it.* (Ecclesiastes
> 7:12)

Wisdom is the first capital requirement in leadership; those who lack it never succeed or fail woefully in the midst of tempest and awful experiences of turbulence.

> *Wisdom is the principal thing; therefore get*
> *wisdom: and with all thy getting get understanding.*
> (Proverbs 4:7)

The worth of wisdom is invaluable and incomparable with all the earthly possessions; those leaders who have wisdom are never in the class of they that amass riches in leadership.

> *For wisdom is better than rubies; and all the things that may be desired are not to be compared to it.* (Proverbs 8:11)

> *How much better is it to get wisdom than gold! And to get understanding rather to be chosen than silver!* (Proverbs 16:16)

Divine wisdom is released unto everyone who desires the truth in the inward part.

> *Behold, thou desirest truth in the inward parts: and in the hidden part thou shalt make me to know wisdom.* (Psalm 51:6)

Nothing teaches wisdom for leadership than the Word of God; nothing also makes a leader prosperous in God than His living Word.

> *This book of the law shall not depart out of thy mouth; but thou shalt meditate therein day and night, that thou mayest observe to do according to all that is written therein: for then thou shalt make thy way prosperous, and then thou shalt have good success.* (Joshua 1:8)

> *The law of the LORD is perfect, converting the soul: the testimony of the LORD is sure, making wise the simple. The statutes of the LORD are right, rejoicing the heart: the commandment of the LORD is pure, enlightening the eyes.* (Proverbs 19:7–8)

The Spirit of God's wisdom is in His knowledge, and not in sensual and general knowledge.

Therefore, where there is no God's knowledge, the Spirit of His wisdom will not be found or be at work.

> *Cease not to give thanks for you, making mention of you in my prayers; That the God of our Lord Jesus Christ, the Father of glory, may give unto you the spirit of wisdom and revelation in the knowledge of him.* (Ephesians 1:16–17)

> *For this cause we also, since the day we heard it, do not cease to pray for you, and to desire that ye might be filled with the knowledge of his will in all wisdom and spiritual understanding.* (Colossians 1:9)

What makes a leader great and unforgettable is wisdom.

> *I communed with mine own heart, saying, "Lo, I am come to great estate, and have gotten more wisdom than all they that have been before me in Jerusalem: yea, my heart had great experience of wisdom and knowledge."* (Ecclesiastes 1:16)

Nothing can be built tangibly or intangibly when a demand of leadership is placed on a person or persons except by spirit of wisdom.

> *Wisdom hath builded her house, she hath hewn out her seven pillars: She hath killed her beasts; she hath mingled her wine; she hath also furnished her table.* (Proverbs 9:1–2)

> *Through wisdom is a house builded; and by understanding it is established.* (Proverbs 24:3)

Divine wisdom births the spirit of prudency, counsel, justice, humility, truth, uprightness, and resilience.

> *Only by pride cometh contention: but with the well advised is wisdom.* (Proverbs 13:10)

> *The wisdom of the prudent is to understand his way: but the folly of fools is deceit.* (Proverbs 14:8)

> *The mouth of the just bringeth forth wisdom: but the froward tongue shall be cut out.* (Proverbs 10:31)

> *When pride cometh, then cometh shame: but with the lowly is wisdom.* (Proverbs 11:2)

> *Folly is joy to him that is destitute of wisdom: but a man of understanding walketh uprightly.* (Proverbs 15:21)

> *Counsel is mine, and sound wisdom: I am understanding; I have strength.* (Proverbs 8:14)

The desire of a man of wisdom is not earthly but in alignment with God's desires.

> *Through desire a man, having separated himself, seeketh and intermeddleth with all wisdom.* (Proverbs 18:1)

A man of divine wisdom never loses his/her peace and is always calm in the face of conflict and leadership challenges.

> *He that is void of wisdom despiseth his neighbour: but a man of understanding holdeth his peace.* (Proverbs 11:12)

Wisdom delivers victory not might.

> *Now there was found in it a poor wise man, and he by his wisdom delivered the city; yet no man remembered that same poor man. "Then," said I, "wisdom is better than strength: nevertheless the poor man's wisdom is despised, and his words are not heard. Wisdom is better than weapons of war."* (Ecclesiastes 9:15–16, 18a)

Leadership without direction will be at the mercy of any occurrence and will travail in endless struggles. It is wisdom that compasses a leader's movement and decision in right direction.

> *If the iron be blunt, and he do not whet the edge, then must he put to more strength: but wisdom is profitable to direct.* (Ecclesiastes 10:10)

A leader gains stability in position of authority by wisdom.

> *And wisdom and knowledge shall be the stability of thy times, and strength of salvation: the fear of the LORD is his treasure.* (Isaiah 33:6)

Divine wisdom distinguishes a man from the crowd and places him above his pairs, foes, and competitors.

> *There is a man in thy kingdom, in whom is the spirit of the holy gods; and in the days of thy father light and understanding and wisdom, like the wisdom of the gods, was found in him; whom the king Nebuchadnezzar thy father, the king, I say, thy father, made master of the magicians, astrologers, Chaldeans, and soothsayers."* (Daniel 5:11)

Jesus Christ Is the Wisdom of God

Jesus Christ is the embodiment of God's wisdom; He is the word and wisdom of God by whom all things were fitly framed and created. The Bible brings to our understanding that:

> But unto them which are called, both Jews and Greeks, Christ the power of God, and the wisdom of God. (1 Corinthians 1:24)

> In the beginning was the Word, and the Word was with God, and the Word was God. The same was in the beginning with God. All things were made by him; and without him was not any thing made that was made. In him was life; and the life was the light of men. And the light shineth in darkness; and the darkness comprehended. (John 1:1–5)

Nothing was made that was not made by wisdom. In Christ is the life of all creations; all the creatures are conditioned by God to secure their existence in Him. He is the light that dispels darkness that daily beclouds and threatens the lives of men.

Without Jesus, leadership failure is imminent; recorded successes, if there are any, will be eroded, and there will more complexities that will rubbish any accomplishment of any leader who has not come to the term that it is God that rules in the affairs of men.

The book of Prophet Isaiah chapter 11 from verse 1 to verse 2 says:

> And there shall come forth a rod out of the stem of Jesse, and a Branch shall grow out of his roots: And the spirit of the LORD shall rest upon him, the spirit of wisdom and understanding, the spirit of counsel and might, the spirit of knowledge and of the fear of the LORD.

And out of the throne proceeded lightnings and thunderings and voices: and there were seven lamps of fire burning before the throne, which are the seven spirits of God. (Revelations 4:5)

The flow pattern of God's seven spirits in Jesus is depicted in the chart diagram below:

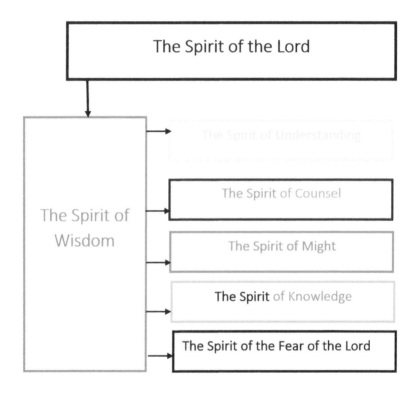

In Jesus is the treasures of divine wisdom and knowledge; He is the wisdom of God, the container of wisdom and giver of it.

In whom are hid all the treasures of wisdom and knowledge. (Colossians 2:3)

There is only one Spirit of God; all the seven spirits are one in the Holy Spirit, and no one can possess one of the seven spirits without others. Jesus is not only our salvation; he is also the perfect example of a leader provided by God to meet the intangible and tangible needs of all men.

Jesus's leadership model is the healing of nations and an eternal way out of human depravities, crises, and woes. In His leadership example lies what will always work among the humans.

Therefore, those who embrace Jesus as God in the son that came to the world to show us what is best in leadership and how best to rule in the affairs of men will raise the bar of requirements for leadership and building it around what Jesus began to do and teach.

> Jesus's leadership model is the healing of nations and an eternal way out of human depravities, crises, and woes. In His leadership example lies what will always work among the humans.

The Spirit of Government

The prophecy of Isaiah (Chapter 11) on the deliverance of Jerusalem from Sennacherib explicitly gives account of Jesus, the Messiah, in a manner that ancient Jews understood the time He was to come; therefore, after their great sufferings, they desired a leader who will avenge their foes and restore their possessions and dignity among other nations of the world.

They had a picture of who they wanted messiah to be: a ruthless, violent, no-nonsense, unforgiving, and blood-thirsty warrior; but unfortunately, Jesus had no comeliness by which anyone could have accepted Him as a leader over them.

The book of Prophet Isaiah 53:2 says, *"For he shall grow up before him as a tender plant, and as a root out of a dry ground: he hath no form nor comeliness; and when we shall see him, there is no beauty that we should desire him."*

Jesus, though coming from a lineage of David, was but from a belittled village of Bethlehem that no one ever thinks can be the birthplace of the Messiah.

> *But thou, Bethlehem Ephratah, though thou*
> *be little among the thousands of Judah, yet out of*
> *thee shall he come forth unto me that is to be ruler*
> *in Israel; whose goings forth have been from of old,*
> *from everlasting.* (Micah 5:2)

The prophecy of Jesus as the Messiah, the leader God sent to deliver Israel, was despised at a time when the people witnessed how he fed over five thousand people with five barley loaves and two small fishes. After the miracle, they wanted to take him by force and crown Him as king, but Jesus went away to avoid it, as recorded in the book of John 6:5 below.

> *When Jesus therefore perceived that they would*
> *come and take him by force, to make him a king,*
> *he departed again into a mountain himself alone.*
> (John 6:5)

The book of Isaiah (Chapter 11) speaks volume about leadership characteristics of Jesus as follows:
Qualifications for His great undertaking (Isaiah 11:1–3):

1. A rod out of the stem of Jesse and a branch. The two words used, a *rod* and a *branch*, signify a weak, small, tender product: a twig and a sprig, such as is easily broken off. (Isaiah 53:2).
2. He is said to come out of Jesse rather than David, because Jesse lived and died in meanness and obscurity; his family was of small account (1 Samuel 18:18), and it was in a way of contempt and reproach that David was sometimes called the son of Jesse. (1 Samuel 22:7).
3. The Spirit of the LORD shall rest upon Him; that is, Holy Spirit in all gifts and grace without measure (Colossians 1:19; 2:9). The Spirit of God endows Jesus with the spirit of government, which is the seal of divine authority upon

Him to execute and succeed in what has been committed into His hand. (John 5:22, 27).

For he whom God hath sent speaketh the words of God: for God giveth not the Spirit by measure unto him. (John 3:34)

The Spirit of God endows Jesus with the spirit of government, which is the seal of divine authority upon Him to execute and succeed in what has been committed into His hand.

4. He shall have the spirit of wisdom and understanding, the spirit of counsel, and the spirit of knowledge. In other words, Jesus shall have thorough understanding of all the dimensions of His leadership's responsibility and shall know how to administer the affairs of governance of His kingdom; He will have treasure of divine wisdom hid in Him to proffer solutions to all problems.

All things are delivered unto me of my Father: and no man knoweth the Son, but the Father; neither knoweth any man the Father, save the Son, and he to whomsoever the Son will reveal him. (Matthew 11:27)

5. He shall have the spirit of might or courage or fortitude, never to give up in the most challenging times, especially upholding the truth and standing for God before men in the face of resistance.

And they sent out unto him their disciples with the Herodians, saying, "Master, we know that thou art true, and teachest the way of God in truth, neither carest thou for any man: for thou regardest not the person of men." (Matthew 22:16)

127

6. God shall make Jesus of quick understanding in the fear of the Lord. The Holy Spirit shall guide His steps to always take right decisions even in the most turbulent periods. He will do everything in reverence to God and consider the instructions and dictates of God in all His deeds, actions, and thoughts. He will be zealous and consumed with passion for the things of God.

7. He shall not judge after the sight of his eyes, neither reprove after the hearing of his ears. His judgments will be based on leading of God and not on external pressures.

> *Behold my servant, whom I uphold; mine elect, in whom my soul delighteth; I have put my spirit upon him: he shall bring forth judgment to the Gentiles.* (Isaiah 42:1)

The justice and equity of his government (Isaiah 11:4–5):

1. But with righteousness shall he judge the poor.
2. Reprove with equity for the meek of the earth.
3. He shall smite the earth with the rod of his mouth, and with the breath of his lips shall he slay the wicked.
4. Righteousness shall be the girdle of his loins.
5. Faithfulness shall be the girdle of his reins

The peace of His kingdom (Isaiah 11:6–9):

One critical pursuit of a godly leader is ensuring peace and pursuing it, working tirelessly to create a calm and secured environment. Where there is no peace, there can never be any progress and development.

What the world organizations mostly expend on is securing the world in peace; the United Nations and other alliances are overwhelmed with conflicts and wars among many nations across the world, but despite their efforts, religious, economy, and territorial wars are still very rampant.

The theories and policies' frameworks of conflicts resolutions continue to fail. What we need is the evolvement of leaders after the heart of God. Only the class of these leaders like Solomon can guarantee peace by the influence of the spirit of wisdom, understanding, and counsel.

> *And the LORD gave Solomon wisdom, as he promised him: and there was peace between Hiram and Solomon; and they two made a league together.* (1 Kings 5:12)

The book of Isaiah 11:6–9 gives description of peace that is attainable by Jesus, the wisdom of God, as follows:

1. *"The wolf also shall dwell with the lamb, and the leopard shall lie down with the kid, the calf and the young lion and the fatling together; and a little child shall lead them."*
2. *"And the cow and the bear shall feed; their young ones shall lie down together: and the lion shall eat straw like the ox."*
3. *"And the sucking child shall play on the hole of the asp, and the weaned child shall put his hand on the cockatrice's den."*
4. *"They shall not hurt nor destroy in all my holy mountain: the earth shall be full of the knowledge of the LORD, as the waters cover the sea."*

Therefore, only the enthroned of the Lord can gain access to wisdom for promotion and achievement of *peace*; no worldly government can attain peace in leadership except by divine leading.

> Jesus says, *"Peace I leave with you, my peace I give unto you: not as the world giveth, give I unto you. Let not your heart be troubled, neither let it be afraid."* (John 4:27)

> *And I will give peace in the land, and ye shall lie down, and none shall make you afraid: and I*

will rid evil beasts out of the land, neither shall the sword go through your land. (Leviticus 26:6)

For brass I will bring gold, and for iron I will bring silver, and for wood brass, and for stones iron: I will also make thy officers peace, and thine exactors righteousness. (Isaiah 60:17)

And this shall be a sign unto you; Ye shall find the babe wrapped in swaddling clothes, lying in a manger. And suddenly there was with the angel a multitude of the heavenly host praising God, and saying, Glory to God in the highest, and on earth peace, good will toward men. (Luke 2:11–14)

And thou, child, shalt be called the prophet of the Highest: for thou shalt go before the face of the Lord to prepare his ways; To give knowledge of salvation unto his people by the remission of their sins, Through the tender mercy of our God; whereby the dayspring from on high hath visited us, To give light to them that sit in darkness and in the shadow of death, to guide our feet into the way of peace. (Luke 1:76–79)

Comparing human wisdom with divine wisdom:

Who is a wise man and endued with knowledge among you? let him shew out of a good conversation his works with meekness of wisdom. But if ye have bitter envying and strife in your hearts, glory not, and lie not against the truth. This wisdom descendeth not from above, but is earthly, sensual, devilish.
For where envying and strife is, there is confusion and every evil work. But the wisdom that is

from above is first pure, then peaceable, gentle, and easy to be intreated, full of mercy and good fruits, without partiality, and without hypocrisy. And the fruit of righteousness is sown in peace of them that make peace. (James 3:13–18)

There is a clear difference between the strength of divine wisdom and human wisdom. Human wisdom or fleshly wisdom is sensual, impure, crafted in selfishness and in the understanding of men, unstable or can be reversed, full of deceits, compounded in foolishness, and above all, can fail.

Divine wisdom is unique, unchangeable by time or season, beyond the understanding of a mortal, is endless and without limit, has life of God in it, is secured, irresistible, endures, and above all, never fails.

The Bible says, *"And they were not able to resist the wisdom and the spirit by which he spake."* (Acts 6:10)

O the depth of the riches both of the wisdom and knowledge of God! how unsearchable are his judgments, and his ways past finding out! (Romans 11:33)

For I will give you a mouth and wisdom, which all your adversaries shall not be able to gainsay nor resist. (Luke 21:15)

For the wisdom of this world is foolishness with God. For it is written, He taketh the wise in their own craftiness. (1 Corinthians 3:19)

Apostle Paul called human wisdom mere:

- excellency of speech or of wisdom;
- word only;

- wisdom of words;
- cunningly devised fables.

(References: 1 Corinthians 1:17; 2:1; 1 Thessalonians 1:5; 2 Peter 1:16.)

There is no replicable human wisdom, but the wisdom of God is multiplicative and eternal. Divine wisdom is characterized by the nature of God and unlimited in application.

Where a leader coordinates the affairs in leadership by wisdom from above, it is without stress and struggles he finds ways out of complexities in governance and with total submission of the lead he enjoys his reign.

Those who think leading men is critically a function of sensual capacity—be it intelligence, brilliancy, and experiences—regret over the so-called men of intellect that are leading them.

> *Where is the wise? where is the scribe? where is the disputer of this world? hath not God made foolish the wisdom of this world?* (1 Corinthians 1:20)

> *Howbeit we speak wisdom among them that are perfect: yet not the wisdom of this world, nor of the princes of this world, that come to nought.* (1 Corinthians 2:6)

Human wisdom generates limited power, but divine wisdom multiplies God's regenerative power.

> *…That your faith should not stand in the wisdom of men, but in the power of God.* (1 Corinthians 2:5)

Earthly wisdom deployment in leadership is like a blind leading the blind; only godly wisdom can provide light unto the path of a leader in order to guide and guard the lead in the way, and only the wisdom from above is needed to straighten the path of leadership.

> *And I will bring the blind by a way that they knew not; I will lead them in paths that they have not known: I will make darkness light before them, and crooked things straight. These things will I do unto them, and not forsake them.* (Isaiah 42:16)

Only the wisdom from above is needed to straighten the path of leadership.

Raising Godly Generation

> Every generation failed to attain the best and to reproduce godly seeds for the next generation because her leaders failed God.

G od plans ahead of time by making provisions for every generation. He raises leaders that will uphold His plans and work unconditionally for the accomplishment of His purpose on earth in every nation.

God is concerned about individuals, families, communities, tribes, and nations, and so He places more demands on who bear rules or govern over them from one generation to another.

Since the earth has been given to men to occupy, angels or any heavenly hosts are not permitted to rule in the affairs of men; God Himself rules in human affairs but through men.

The book of Genesis 1:27–28 says: *"So God created man in his own image, in the image of God created he him; male and female created he them. And God blessed them, and God said unto them, 'Be fruitful, and multiply, and replenish the earth, and subdue it: and have dominion over the fish of the sea, and over the fowl of the air, and over every living thing that moveth upon the earth.'"*

Therefore, it is the duty of men to make the earth a habitable place by aligning with the raising and placing of godly leaders in charge of affairs of men. In other words, men are largely responsible for the choice of leaders over them.

The requirements of God for a choice of leaders are the same all over the world. Since families are togetherness of individuals, communities are coming-together of families, families constitute a nation of different tribes and languages, nations constitute a country, and coming-together of people of different countries constitute a continent. We can say that leadership provides them is largely responsible for their woes and conflicts as well as their prosperity and development.

Except we follow after the pattern of God in raising godly men across all nations of people; bad leaders will continue to thrive and dominate the domains of men.

The biblical truth of raising godly leaders is as follows:

> *Even so every good tree bringeth forth good fruit; but a corrupt tree bringeth forth evil fruit. A good tree cannot bring forth evil fruit, neither can a corrupt tree bring forth good fruit.* (Matthew 7:17–18)

The biblical verses above imply that every seed produces its kind. Therefore, leadership has a nature of being replicable, repeatable, reproducible, and multipliable. In other words, a leader will always produce his/her kinds that can continue to be in charge of his domain.

*****

The first biblical focus in raising a godly generation of leaders is parents. The first parents in the Bible, Adam and Eve, were responsible for who Cain and Abel were. Some of the questions one may ask include:

- How did they raise Cain and Abel?
- Why was Abel different from Cain, and what was responsible?
- What went wrong with Adam and Eve's value system that led to how Cain turned out?

- Should we hold Cain and Abel responsible for what befell them?
- Were there any external influences on Abel and Cain?

It is clear that Adam and Eve were wired by God with His nature, for the Bible says, *"They were created in God's image."* God gave them everything to be able to influence their children in His ways but, directly or indirectly, raised a leader in Cain that hunted them till they died.

God breathed onto Adam, and he became a living soul; and Eve, who was made from Adam's bone, had the nature of God too. Therefore, parenthood and parenting and their understanding from God's instructions and injunctions are the first and primary source and foundation of raising godly generation.

Every society originates from families that are constituted by fathers and mothers.

Parenthood and Parenting

A father and a mother are the first leaders raised by God to occupy, replenish, and multiply the earth; and as such, the type of leaders they are or what their leadership inclinations are will continually have positive or negative effects on their kinds they reproduce to fill the earth.

Parenthood—the state of being a parent, and the responsibilities involved—and parenting, the activity of bringing up a child as a parent, are crucial to who the children become.

God's expectation from the beginning is that parents teach their children the way to go; in other words, no one influences children better than their parents; that is, what a child eventually becomes is a function of how he/she was raised.

> Lo, children are an heritage of the LORD: and the fruit of the womb is his reward. As arrows are in the hand of a mighty man; so are children of the youth.

Happy is the man that hath his quiver full of them: they shall not be ashamed, but they shall speak with the enemies in the gate. (Psalm 127:3–5)

There is a battle for the souls of the children by God and the devil, and so, God expects parents to raise them in the way of the Lord to become instruments in His hand against the devil.

Remember, if parents fail to teach their children in the best way to go, because of their curiosity to know, they will become learners in the hand of the devil.

There is no settlement of people in any part of the world that does not have history of its progenitors; that is, the first human settlers. Therefore, the demand of leadership rests upon the shoulders of these great men and women who had lived at a time before they began to multiply in numbers.

Who these first settlers were and their understanding about God speak volumes of how they were able to provide direction in leadership for their children and servants/maids.

Parents that do not know God and His demand on them, though may be working hard, labor in vain to raise another generation of people who will take after them. In other words, their failure in training and imbibing the fear of God and tenets of human responsibilities to God and others always result into the evolvement of untrustworthy men in leadership.

Even though progenitors of many nations may not be as educated or lettered as we are now, or they may not be sophisticated as we are now, they do not have an excuse for failing their generation because God did prepare them for the challenges of their time. The world they were at that time, in its forms of complexity, was not beyond the deposit of God's wisdom, intellect, strength, and ability in them.

This is the instruction of God to parents in raising godly generations:

And thou shalt love the LORD thy God with all thine heart, and with all thy soul, and with all thy might. And these words, which I command thee this day, shall be in thine heart: And thou shalt teach them diligently unto thy children, and shalt talk of them when thou sittest in thine house, and when thou walkest by the way, and when thou liest down, and when thou risest up.

And thou shalt bind them for a sign upon thine hand, and they shall be as frontlets between thine eyes. And thou shalt write them upon the posts of thy house, and on thy gates. (Deuteronomy 6:5–9)

Where parents do not know God, their offspring will be children of rebellion against the Lord. In other words, no parents can give what they do not have. And when the parents love the Lord with all their heart, soul, and might, God emphasizes their continuous influence over their children by:

- diligently teaching their children;
- by talking to them when sitting together in the house, when they walk together by the way, when they are about to lie down or to sleep, and when they wake up;
- by living a life of example in deeds, in actions, and in words;
- by a clear and defining culture, and principles of Godliness in all their relationship with them

Proverbs 22:6 says, *"Train up a child in the way he should go: and when he is old, he will not depart from it."*

Therefore, because children are great imitators with very high intelligent quotient and retentive memory, leading them by the right part from the beginning gives them an advantage in becoming an arrow and instrument in the hand of the Lord to liberate other people from all bondages and provide godly leadership.

Queen Esther and Cyrus, the King of Persia

After the dethronement of Queen Vashti by King Ahasuerus, the Xerxes who ruled over 127 provinces from his royal throne in the citadel of Susa stretching from India to Cush, Esther—an orphan and a captive Jewess who had lost her parents—became the Queen and gave birth to Cambyses, who happened to be the mother of King Cyrus of Persia in Babylon.

Queen Esther's daughter, Cambyses, was raised by her mother in all diligence, and that acquainted her to know the God of the Jews. Cambyses was raised in opulence and wealth at the palace of Xerxes but was subjected to the fear of the Lord from infant.

Cambyses, the daughter of Queen Esther, in turn also imparted in her son, Cyrus, the knowledge and fear of Yahweh. Cyrus grew up with a reverence heart to the God of all flesh; he became the choice of God's leader to liberate the Israelites from bondage.

The prophecies of prophets Isaiah and Jeremiah concerning Cyrus are pointers to the truth that Cyrus was never against God of Israel, and neither was he an idolater nor a king God never trusted.

Let us examine some of the biblical records on Cyrus:

> *Now in the first year of Cyrus king of Persia, that the word of the LORD spoken by the mouth of Jeremiah might be accomplished, the LORD stirred up the spirit of Cyrus, king of Persia, that he made a proclamation throughout all his kingdom, and put it also in writing, saying,*
>
> *Thus saith Cyrus, king of Persia, "All the kingdoms of the earth hath the LORD God of heaven given me; and he hath charged me to build him an house in Jerusalem, which is in Judah. Who is there among you of all his people? The LORD his God be with him, and let him go up."* (2 Chronicles 36:22–23)
>
> *That saith of Cyrus, He is my shepherd, and shall perform all my pleasure: even saying to*

Jerusalem, Thou shalt be built; and to the temple, Thy foundation shall be laid. (Isaiah 44:28)

Thus saith the LORD to his anointed, "To Cyrus, whose right hand I have holden, to subdue nations before him; and I will loose the loins of kings, to open before him the two leaved gates; and the gates shall not be shut;
"I will go before thee, and make the crooked places straight: I will break in pieces the gates of brass, and cut in sunder the bars of iron: And I will give thee the treasures of darkness, and hidden riches of secret places, that thou mayest know that I, the LORD, which call thee by thy name, am the God of Israel." (Isaiah 45:1–3)

(Other references: Ezra 1:1–11; 5:13–14; 6:3.)

Cyrus—King of Persia—though was raised from the far east in Babylon, the truth is that he encountered God of Israel; he was God's servant. He always hears from God for direction, and he lived at his time to fulfill the divine mandate over Israel.

The notion of many people has been that Cyrus was an idolater since he reigned over Babylon, but that was far from the truth. It is on record in the book of Ezra 1:2–3 that *"Thus saith Cyrus king of Persia, 'The LORD God of heaven hath given me all the kingdoms of the earth; and he hath charged me to build him an house at Jerusalem, which is in Judah. Who is there among you of all his people? His God be with him, and let him go up to Jerusalem, which is in Judah, and build the house of the LORD God of Israel, (he is God,) which is in Jerusalem.'"*

And this implies Cyrus's deeper knowledge of God for being trained from infancy by his mother, Cambyses; and when he grew up, he did not depart from it.

The use of the words "God stirred up his spirit," "He is my shepherd," and "whose right hand I have holden to subdue nations before him" on Cyrus from above scriptures were not arbitrarily used;

they are proofs that Cyrus knew God even before he became king of Persia.

If Cyrus was not a man who feared the Lord, the use of the word "God hardened his heart" because of his stiff-neckedness to fulfill the prophecy of rebuilding Jerusalem would have been used.

In all generations where parents are far away from God or where parents rejected God to lead, guide, and direct their paths, the leadership they provide gives birth to generations of leaders without the fear of God: men in whom there is no reverence for God and people; leaders who are desperately wicked, unrighteous, lovers of self, inconsiderate and merciless; and rulers who work continuously against the counsel of the Lord and the peace of the governed.

The book of Deuteronomy 4:9 concerning parenting says, *"Only take heed to thyself, and keep thy soul diligently, lest thou forget the things which thine eyes have seen, and lest they depart from thy heart all the days of thy life: but teach them thy sons, and thy sons' sons."*

When parents are not first the example, the source of knowledge and inspiration for their children, it becomes very easy for the devil through other mediums to lead the innocent children in a way that leads to destruction.

Parental guidance to raise godly generation of leaders is also rooted in discipline.

Discipline is a form of teaching and informally educating children on what is worth living for and how to live a worthy life. Discipline demands strictness, bluntness, punitive measures, rewards for good conducts, consistency, and exemplary living on the part of the parents.

Parents with low or compromising moral standard will not be able to achieve much in raising godly generation of children.

The Bible says:

> *Withhold not correction from the child: for if thou beatest him with the rod, he shall not die. Thou shalt beat him with the rod, and shalt deliver his soul from hell.* (Proverbs 23:13–14)

A child's heart has a tendency to do wrong, but the rod of discipline removes it far away from him. (Proverbs 22:15)

The rod and rebuke bestow wisdom, but an undisciplined child brings shame to his mother. Discipline your child, and he will give you rest; he will bring you happiness. (Proverbs 29:15, 17)

In the course of raising godly generation of leaders among children, discipline must be regulated not to the extreme of misuse of its power to inflict emotional burden, psychological trauma, and loss of self-confidence in them.

When discipline becomes an instrument to hunt down, to ridicule, or to exercise undue advantage over the children, they will grow up with identity crisis, become fearful to face challenges, may lose strength to forge ahead, and become unprepared for leadership.

Excessive and unregulated discipline causes children to stumble, thereby hardening their hearts against corrections and rebuke. Discipline must be deployed with love and in love, and not with utter mindset of condemnation.

Scriptural passages that warn parents of taking discipline to the extreme are:

Fathers, provoke not your children to anger, lest they be discouraged. (Colossians 3:21)

Parents, do not anger your children, but rear them in the discipline and in the teaching of Our Lord. (Ephesians 6:4)

But you must see to it that this right of yours does not become a stumbling block for those who are weak. (1 Corinthians 8:9)

Parental guidance to raise godly generation of leaders is also rooted in exemplary life.

Our generation has a large number of parents who just want to give order to their children without being an example unto them. But we know that children learn more from parents' actions; therefore, the Bible says, "a bad tree cannot produce a good fruit, and neither can a good tree produce a bad fruit." The seeds parents are planting in the lives of their children must grow first in their lives before they grow in their children's lives.

> *Feed the flock of God which is among you, taking the oversight thereof, not by constraint, but willingly; not for filthy lucre, but of a ready mind; Neither as being lords over God's heritage, but being ensamples to the flock.* (1 Peter 5:2–3)

> *For so is the will of God, that with well doing ye may put to silence the ignorance of foolish men.* (1 Peter 2:15)

> *For our gospel came not unto you in word only, but also in power, and in the Holy Ghost, and in much assurance; as ye know what manner of men we were among you for your sake. And ye became followers of us, and of the Lord, having received the word in much affliction, with joy of the Holy Ghost: So that ye were ensamples to all that believe in Macedonia and Achaia.* (1 Thessalonians 1:5–7)

The Bible says in Matthew 5:15–16 that *"people don't light a lamp and put it under a basket but on a lamp stand, and it gives light to everyone in the house. In the same way, let your light shine in front of people. Then they will see the good that you do and praise your Father in heaven."*

No one can be raised beyond the exemplary lifestyle he is exposed to; therefore, children grasp more from their parents' lifestyle than what they have being taught.

Divine Mandate for the Church in Raising Godly Generation

The church is the voice of God to rebuke, warn, correct, and stabilize every nation under God by raising people of impeccable characters who God can trust in leading others.

Church is the ground and pillar of truth entrusted by God to bequeath godly values and culture for living to all men.

The judgement of God over the earth and its inhabitants will begin at the Church because it is in her that He has invested all of Himself to liberate the world and make it a better place to live.

It has been long that societies and worldly system have been failing in meeting God's expectations in preserving the world a peaceful habitation of men and women whose reason for living is to please God; organize it; provide godly leadership; and raise generations of faithful, resilient, upright, and selfless people that can be counted upon by God in His quest to make the world a better place.

> *God looked down from heaven upon the children of men, to see if there were any that did understand, that did seek God.* (Psalm 53:2)

There is no world system that can be trusted at this time to meet the demand of God for raising godly generation.

The depravity, the ungodliness, the wickedness, and the rebellion of nations of men in our generation and previous ones are worse than the days of Sodom and Gomorrah. From the time immemorial, God had a plan to deliver the world from the cloak of darkness that is making men to revolt against Him in order to set a standard for themselves against the purpose of God for all human races.

In the old and new testaments through God's ministers—prophets, kings, apostles, pastors, and other leaders of people who He planted in leadership—God sets standards of how people should live, cohabit, and lead others. This move of God provided sanity and instilled fear in many people of the old and new covenants in order for the purpose of God for man not to be truncated.

Prophets like Elijah, Elisha, Nathan, Samuel, Jeremiah, Ezekiel, Isaiah, Deborah, Micah; leaders of great repute like Abraham; Sarah; Moses; Joshua; Caleb; Hezekiah; Nehemiah; John the Baptist; Stephen; Simon; Peter; Ruth; Mary; Martha; Mary Magdalene; Priscilla; Dorcas; Elizabeth; King Asa; King Cyrus; King David; etc. were heralded into positions of leadership with strict and absolute instructions from God on how to lead people on God's own terms.

And when any of these leaders raised by God defaulted, He dealt with them in the standard of His call upon their lives without a respect for anyone than another.

For reference purposes, Psalm 77:20 says, *"Thou leddest thy people like a flock by the hand of Moses and Aaron,"* but when they erred from God's dictates, the same Bible says:

> *Moses and Aaron among his priests, and Samuel among them that call upon his name; they called upon the LORD, and he answered them. He spake unto them in the cloudy pillar: they kept his*

testimonies, and the ordinance that he gave them.
Thou answeredst them, O LORD our God: thou wast
a God that forgavest them, though thou tookest ven-
geance of their inventions. (Psalm 99:6–8)

The political, educational, and the economic systems of the world continue to spell doom for the world; in fact, there is more confusion and palpable fear among the inhabitants of the world at this time than before.

Therefore, God raised Jesus to bring together a people of diverse color and race to the knowledge of who God is and to raise a new generation of people the world never knew; people who, though are in the world, carve a new world of Jesus's reign among men.

Right from the ancient times, God had always raised leaders who were blessings and not a curse to their generations; but His ultimate plan is to call, develop, and empower these people in all generations who will stand out for God after they have been regenerated to have their nature transformed to the nature of Jesus Christ.

These new generations of men are regenerated beings who consciously work away from worldliness to please God and dominate or occupy for Him until His second coming. They are men, women, and children who have encountered the Savior of the world, Jesus; they now have the nature of Christ in them to overcome worldly temptations in all forms.

They are a population of men whom God has prepared through personal encounter with the greatest leader, the firstborn among the living and the death.

Who is the image of the invisible God, the
firstborn of every creature: For by him were all
things created, that are in heaven, and that are in
earth, visible and invisible, whether they be thrones,
or dominions, or principalities, or powers: all things
were created by him, and for him:
And he is before all things, and by him all
things consist. And he is the head of the body, the

> *church: who is the beginning, the firstborn from the*
> *dead; that in all things he might have the preemi-*
> *nence. For it pleased the Father that in him should*
> *all fulness dwell.* (Colossians 1:15–18)

Jesus was there with God from the beginning; He is the first-born of God, and so He knows what people should be empowered with to lead others.

When Jesus came, He raised a team of leaders through His doctrines and how He lived to reorientate them about the desires, expectations, requirements, and demands of God in leadership.

There is no one who ever lived or is living who was and is a leader like Jesus. The Bible says:

> *God, who at sundry times and in divers*
> *manners spake in time past unto the fathers by the*
> *prophets, Hath in these last days spoken unto us by*
> *his Son, whom he hath appointed heir of all things,*
> *by whom also he made the worlds;*
> *Who being the brightness of his glory, and the*
> *express image of his person, and upholding all things*
> *by the word of his power, when he had by himself*
> *purged our sins, sat down on the right hand of the*
> *Majesty on high;*
> *Being made so much better than the angels,*
> *as he hath by inheritance obtained a more excellent*
> *name than they.* (Hebrews 1:1–4)

And so the team of disciples Jesus raised became the first set of leaders He commissioned to multiply and reproduce their kinds across all nations of the world. This team of disciples excluded Judas Iscariot that made it to a leadership commission first called the Church.

> *…And when he had found him, he brought*
> *him unto Antioch. And it came to pass, that a whole*

year they assembled themselves with the church, and
taught much people. And the disciples were called
Christians first in Antioch. (Acts 1:26)

The people that constitute the church are people from all over
the world who are willing to admit and acknowledge their depravity,
woes, unworthiness, weaknesses, wickedness, inadequacies, inability,
and emptiness, and trade them at the feet of Jesus for a new birth
or rebirth; salvation and deliverance; regeneration; a new character;
unpolluted wisdom; and a new way of life so that they can live to
please God and know His ways and how to walk therein.

The people who surrender unto Jesus become saved from beg-
garly elements of this world that easily turn them to rebel against
God. Therefore, until a man is genuinely saved, he/she can never
possess divine ability to lead others for God.

The church, which has Jesus as her head, has been commissioned to turn out millions of men who will be submitting their own
will to run their affairs in life to God's will.

Everyone is saved to lead directly or indirectly; the church is a
divine institution to raise leaders not in the order of any man but in
the order of Jesus Christ.

The Bible says:

> *Therefore, as the church is subject unto Christ,*
> *so let the wives be to their own husbands in every-*
> *thing.* (Ephesians 5:24)

> *But if I tarry long, that thou mayest know how*
> *thou oughtest to behave thyself in the house of God,*
> *which is the church of the living God, the pillar and*
> *ground of the truth.* (Ephesians 5:24)

Church is not about edifices of any design; it is a gathering of
two or more people, or better says it is all about people being raised
in the full knowledge of God through Jesus Christ.

Church is about building people on the foundation of the truth, justice, equity, Godliness: righteousness and holiness; servanthood; accountability, transparency, etc.

The church is the ground and pillar of truth. Church is the only uncompromising institution (even though there are compromising men who are part of the church) for imbibing the tenets of godly leadership that cannot be twisted; one leader raised in this environment will do great exploits in his/her generation incomparably to what millions of worldly inclined and developed leaders will ever do.

The Church of Jesus Christ is beyond the four corners of her wall or just to gather people to worship. It is about raising godly people to occupy every stratum of society for God. The leaders being raised at Church are not only to operate within the church walls. The church altar is also in the marketplace in politics, in science, in research, in business, in engineering, in medicine, in education, in community, in government, in economy, etc.

The purpose of God for the church is to build leaders after His heart to be in charge of human and immaterial resources management, and until this is the testimony across nations and across all human activities, wicked and unworthy men will continue to bear rule over human race.

> The church is the ground and pillar of truth. Church is the only uncompromising institution (even though there are compromising men who are part of the Church) for imbibing the tenets of godly leadership that cannot be twisted; one leader raised in this environment will do great exploits in his/her generation incomparably to what millions of worldly inclined and developed leaders will ever do.

The church enjoys the revelation of manifold wisdom of God to provide critical leadership at the most turbulent period. The Bible says, *"... To the intent that now unto the principalities and powers in heavenly places might be known by the church the manifold wisdom of God"* (Ephesians 3:10).

God will not do anything to meet the needs of all men in leadership except through the church. There is a mystery behind successful leadership, and this is why Apostle Paul wrote in the Bible that:

> *Whereof I was made a minister, according to the gift of the grace of God given unto me by the effectual working of his power. Unto me, who am less than the least of all saints, is this grace given, that I should preach among the Gentiles the unsearchable riches of Christ; And to make all men see what is the fellowship of the mystery, which from the beginning of the world hath been hid in God, who created all things by Jesus Christ.* (Ephesians 3:7–9)

The word *minister* in the above Bible passage means "a leader." Apostle Paul was a different leader to different people in meeting the need of providing godly leadership; He was an educationist, a counselor, a political figure, a community leader, a minister of the gospel of Christ, an evangelist, an entrepreneur, etc. This is what Apostle Paul says:

> *For though I be free from all men, yet have I made myself servant unto all, that I might gain the more. And unto the Jews I became as a Jew, that I might gain the Jews; to them that are under the law, as under the law, that I might gain them that are under the law;*
> *To them that are without law, as without law, (being not without law to God, but under the law to Christ,) that I might gain them that are without law. To the weak became I as weak, that I might gain the weak: I am made all things to all men, that I might by all means save some. And this I do for the gospel's sake, that I might be partaker thereof with you.* (1 Corinthians 9:19–23)

The Core Responsibility of the Church of God

1. Locate unsaved people and bring them to Christ;
2. Teach and educate them in the ways of Christ;
3. Continually watch over the people for monitoring, rebuke, and correction in love;
4. Build in people new character and attitudes aligned to Jesus Christ's.
5. Prepare them for leadership;
6. Launch them into the world to occupy for Jesus in every stratum of human existence;
7. Continually develop the leaders to achieve improvement;
8. Commission them to multiply or reproduce their kinds;
9. Be louder and conscious in preparing the leaders for God's kingdom;
10. Be the voice of God against injustice, inequality, segregation, bad leadership, and every form of ungodliness.

It is ridiculous that our generation of churches is more focused on acquiring and investing in corruptible things than building men to discover God, discover themselves, and be prepared for leadership.

Our understanding of what church is established for is at variance with the original purpose; most people see church as a place of raising heavenly-bound Christians to become pastors, evangelists, etc.; but it is more than that. Church is to take over the earth for God, as the Bible says, *"For the earth will be filled with the knowledge of the glory of the LORD, as the waters cover the sea."* (Habakkuk 2:14)

The Bible in the parable of Jesus says:

> He said therefore, *"A certain nobleman went into a far country to receive for himself a kingdom, and to return."* And he called his ten servants, and delivered them ten pounds, and said unto them, *"Occupy till I come."* (Luke 19:12–13)

The church of God is empowered to raise people who will provide godly leadership in every sphere of life. These men and women hold their positions in trust for God. They are to occupy for Jesus until He comes back.

When the church of God fails to be a role model of godly leadership, the situations in the world will get worse. In this time and season, there have been compromises by the church setting aside the demands of God in leadership to the extent that within her domain, sacred responsibilities are being handled by unholy men.

The sons of Belial are mostly revered; the people that cannot lead their homefronts are at the council of decision-making. Even though all the church assemblies may not be guilty, a damage done by one member of the body of Christ is damage done to others.

The church is the ground and pillar of truth, and so God is holding her responsible for what is going wrong in every strata of leadership. The church is the voice of God to rebuke, warn, correct, and stabilize every nation under God by raising people of impeccable characters who God can trust in leading others.

> *For the time is come that judgment must begin at the house of God: and if it first begin at us, what shall the end be of them that obey not the gospel of God?* (1 Peter 4:17)

The instruction of God to Moses was very clear when He asked him to raise seventy leaders:

> *And the LORD said unto Moses, "Gather unto me seventy men of the elders of Israel, whom thou knowest to be the elders of the people, and officers over them; and bring them unto the tabernacle of the congregation, that they may stand there with thee.*
>
> *And I will come down and talk with thee there: and I will take of the spirit which is upon thee, and will put it upon them; and they shall bear the burden of the people with thee, that thou bear*

it not thyself alone."...And the LORD came down in a cloud, and spake unto him, and took of the spirit that was upon him, and gave it unto the seventy elders: and it came to pass, that, when the spirit rested upon them, they prophesied, and did not cease. (Exodus 24: 16–17, 25)

God raised the seventy leaders to bear the burden of His people unlike what is predominant in leadership in our world, where the leads bear the responsibilities of leadership and the burdens of the leaders.

Divinity upon the World System of Government

> Every leader or everyone in leadership position is first accountable to God and secondly to men, and will give account of his/her stewardship to Him at the end.

Who has bewitched people in leadership? Who could have been deceiving leaders at all levels that leadership is not God's business? Who among leaders are saying whatever they do on earth ends there? What does leaders of men and managers of earthly resources think about the place of God in the affairs of men? Do all men not understand that everyone came from God and shall return to God to give account of their stewardship on earth?

How can leaders think that the creator of the heaven and earth will not be interested in the works of His hand? It seems the leaders who bear responsibilities over people either responsibly or irresponsibly have forgotten that everything is laid bare open before the Lord.

The system of the world, whether favorable or unfavorable and whether godly or ungodly, is going to be judged at the end by God.

There is no leadership provided among men that will not at the end be subjected to God's final judgment.

The Bible says,

> *And he saith unto me, "Seal not the sayings of the prophecy of this book: for the time is at hand. He*

that is unjust, let him be unjust still: and he which is filthy, let him be filthy still: and he that is righteous, let him be righteous still: and he that is holy, let him be holy still. And, behold, I come quickly; and my reward is with me, to give every man according as his work shall be." (Revelations 22:12)

God places more responsibility on leaders of men at all times; He holds them accountable for what transpires and happens to people under their watch. Because every person may find himself/herself in position that demands providing leadership, God sees every man as his/her brother's keeper; therefore, it is not until a position of leadership is occupied before a responsibility of leading others may be placed on someone's shoulder.

Cain was a senior brother to Abel, and so by that position, God sees Cain as a leader to Abel. The Bible says, *"And the LORD said unto Cain, 'Where is Abel thy brother?' And he said, 'I know not: Am I my brother's keeper?'"* (Genesis 4:9).

God held the forefathers of Israel responsible for the woes and disobedience of the people of Israel; He never spared them whether all of them or few played direct or indirect roles in what befell their nation.

The book of Amos 2:4 says, *"Thus saith the LORD, 'For three transgressions of Judah, and for four, I will not turn away the punishment thereof; because they have despised the law of the LORD, and have not kept his commandments, and their lies caused them to err, after the which their fathers have walked.'"*

The book of Ezekiel 20:30, 33 says, *"Wherefore say unto the house of Israel? Thus saith the Lord GOD, 'Are ye polluted after the manner of your fathers? And commit ye whoredom after their abominations?... 'As I live,' saith the Lord GOD, 'surely with a mighty hand, and with a stretched out arm, and with fury poured out will I rule over you.'"*

God placed responsibility of providing direction for His people on the fathers of Israel, but they failed; and this brought woes unto their land.

The truth about God's position on leadership is that someone or a number of people will be held responsible from time to time over human race because He has put men in charge of the works of His hand.

All deeds of men, whether in the light or in the dark, shall be brought to judgment by God as a head of a home, as a boss in the office, as a minister of God, as a wife, as a political leader, as a community leader, as a business owner, as children, and as an individual—all have their domains of providing leadership which they must give account to their creator.

The Bible is very clear that *"For God shall bring every work into judgment, with every secret thing, whether it be good, or whether it be evil."* (Ecclesiastes 12:14). And 2 Corinthians 5:10 says, *"For we must all appear before the judgment seat of Christ; that every one may receive the things done in his body, according to that he hath done, whether it be good or bad."*

> *But he that doeth wrong shall receive for the wrong which he hath done: and there is no respect of persons.* (Colossians 3:25)

We are all accountable to God though, more than one another, depending on His purpose for our lives, the position of authorities we occupy, and the domain of leadership we function in.

God will hold parents responsible for their wards; ministers of God will be held responsible for their followers; political leaders will give account of their domain of leadership; the kings and other community leaders will not escape God's assessment of their use of authority over their subjects.

There are leaders who have been raised above bar of leadership credence but whom God detests. They are celebrated men and women in every stratum of leadership that God abhorred or abhorreth.

There are uncelebrated men and women across the world whose leadership virtues and accomplishments gladden the heart of God. But in all, God will bring every work of darkness or every work in the light unto final judgment.

Be warned, God is watching and taking records of how you live and how your life affects others. God resists the wicked, the ungodly, and selfish people in leadership; He fights them, disgraces them, and frustrates them in all they do, except they yield to God's expectations in leadership. God sees every wrong people in leadership as His enemies; He fights with everything to rescue the oppressed and the suppressed.

> *Thou hast rebuked the heathen, thou hast destroyed the wicked, thou hast put out their name for ever and ever. O thou enemy, destructions are come to a perpetual end: and thou hast destroyed cities; their memorial is perished with them.*
>
> *But the LORD shall endure forever: he hath prepared his throne for judgment. And he shall judge the world in righteousness, he shall minister judgment to the people in uprightness. The LORD also will be a refuge for the oppressed, a refuge in times of trouble.* (Psalm 9:6–9)

There is no degree of subtlety, deception, lies, and pretention in leadership that is not known unto God; no philanthropic gesture can be a covering for any form of wickedness toward the lead.

The Bible says:

> *"Am I a God at hand," saith the LORD, "And not a God afar off? Can any hide himself in secret places that I shall not see him?" saith the LORD. "Do not I fill heaven and earth?" saith the LORD.* (Jeremiah 23:23–24)

Therefore, whatever you are made of in leadership that is never known to anyone who you superintend over is recorded with God; there is no escape route for the wicked, for all shall face judgment of God.

And for those who had misused opportunities of being leaders and had built a secured fortune or future or status or name for themselves but have not repented or make restitutions, their end will be regrettable—what they have built will eventually be destroyed; what they have gathered through unrighteousness will suddenly finish without recovery.

The misrule of Nebuchadnezzar, King of Babylon, was fiercely rewarded by God to warn anyone in leadership position that he/she is privileged from above and has a duty to bear rule over men in accordance with God's ways and expectations.

The book of Daniel 4:30–33 says: *"The king spake, and said, 'Is not this great Babylon, that I have built for the house of the kingdom by the might of my power, and for the honour of my majesty?' While the word was in the king's mouth, there fell a voice from heaven, saying, 'O king Nebuchadnezzar, to thee it is spoken; The kingdom is departed from thee.*

'And they shall drive thee from men, and thy dwelling shall be with the beasts of the field: they shall make thee to eat grass as oxen, and seven times shall pass over thee, until thou know that the most High ruleth in the kingdom of men, and giveth it to whomsoever he will.' The same hour was the thing fulfilled upon Nebuchadnezzar: and he was driven from men, and did eat grass as oxen, and his body was wet with the dew of heaven, till his hairs were grown like eagles' feathers, and his nails like birds' claws."

> *After the demise of Nebuchadnezzar, Belshazzar his son ruled in his place. And in one of its banquets, he saw fingers of a man's hand, and wrote over against the candlestick upon the plaster of the wall of the king's palace: and the king saw the part of the hand that wrote. What was written is "MENE, MENE, TEKEL, UPHARSIN."*
>
> *The interpretation given by Daniel is "This is the interpretation of the thing: MENE; God hath numbered thy kingdom, and finished it. TEKEL; Thou art weighed in the balances, and art found wanting. PERES; Thy kingdom is divided, and given to the Medes and Persians."* (Daniel 5:5, 13–26)

There are many ungodly men in leadership who had escaped being prosecuted by law or held accountable by men because of their grip on power but will never escape the judgment of God. Whether a leader wriggled himself out of being cut by the law or people, he may never live to enjoy what he has acquired even here on earth. The Bible says there is no peace for the wicked.

The book of Psalm 73:2–20 explains it all: How the righteous feels about the wicked in leadership; who wicked and ungodly people or leaders are; and the end of the wicked leaders, and what God will do against them.

How the righteous feels about the wicked in leadership:

1. *"But as for me, my feet were almost gone; my steps had well-nigh slipped.*
2. *"For I was envious at the foolish, when I saw the prosperity of the wicked.*
3. *"For there are no bands in their death: but their strength is firm.*
4. *"They are not in trouble as other men; neither are they plagued like other men.*
5. *"Therefore pride compasseth them about as a chain; violence covereth them as a garment.*
6. *"Their eyes stand out with fatness: they have more than heart could wish."*

Who wicked and ungodly people or leaders are:

1. *"They are corrupt and speak wickedly concerning oppression: they speak loftily.*
2. *"They set their mouth against the heavens, and their tongue walketh through the earth.*
3. *"Therefore his people return hither: and waters of a full cup are wrung out to them.*
4. *"And they say, 'How doth God know? And is there knowledge in the most High?'*
5. *"Behold, these are the ungodly, who prosper in the world; they increase in riches.*
6. *"Verily I have cleansed my heart in vain and washed my hands in innocence.*
7. *"For all the day long have I been plagued, and chastened every morning.*

8. *"If I say, I will speak thus; behold, I should offend against the generation of thy children.*

9. *"When I thought to know this, it was too painful for me."*

The end of the wicked people or leaders, and what God will do against them:

1. *"Until I went into the sanctuary of God; then understood their end.*

2. *"Surely, thou didst set them in slippery places: thou castedst them down into destruction.*

3. *"How are they brought into desolation, as in a moment! they are utterly consumed with terrors.*

4. *"As a dream when one awaketh; so, O Lord, when thou awakest, thou shalt despise their image."*

The Damned Consequences of Ungodly Leaders and Leadership

And I said, "Hear, I pray you, O heads of Jacob, and ye princes of the house of Israel; Is it not for you to know judgment?

"Who hate the good, and love the evil; who pluck off their skin from off them, and their flesh from off their bones.

"Who also eat the flesh of my people, and flay their skin from off them; and they break their bones, and chop them in pieces, as for the pot, and as flesh within the caldron."

Then shall they cry unto the LORD, "But he will not hear them: he will even hide his face from them at that time, as they have behaved themselves ill in their doings."

Thus saith the LORD, "Concerning the prophets that make my people err, that bite with their teeth, and cry, Peace; and he that putteth not into their mouths, they even prepare war against him.

"Therefore night shall be unto you, that ye shall not have a vision; and it shall be dark unto you, that ye shall not divine; and the sun shall go down over the prophets, and the day shall be dark over them.

"Then shall the seers be ashamed, and the diviners confounded: yea, they shall all cover their lips; for there is no answer of God.

"But truly I am full of power by the spirit of the LORD, and of judgment, and of might, to declare unto Jacob his transgression, and to Israel his sin.

"Hear this, I pray you, ye heads of the house of Jacob, and princes of the house of Israel, that abhor judgment, and pervert all equity.

"They build up Zion with blood, and Jerusalem with iniquity.

"The heads thereof judge for reward, and the priests thereof teach for hire, and the prophets thereof divine for money: yet will they lean upon the LORD, and say, 'Is not the LORD among us? None evil can come upon us.'

"Therefore shall Zion for your sake be plowed as a field, and Jerusalem shall become heaps, and the mountain of the house as the high places of the forest." (Micah 3:1–12)

Leadership Woes

The meaning of woe, among many others, include big problems or troubles, extreme sadness, difficult situations, and unpleasant experiences—which may be expressed idiomatically as "heavy cross to bear"; "a fate worse than death"; "a hard/tough row to hoe"; or misery, distress, sorrow, etc.

The failure in leadership due to wickedness and every form of ungodliness is bound to attract untoward experience of woes in the lives of the leaders in question.

What may attract woes to leaders and their leadership is stated in the Word of God as follows:

When leaders are in position for self at the expense of the people:

> *Woe to thee, Moab! thou art undone, O people of Chemosh: he hath given his sons that escaped, and his daughters, into captivity unto Sihon king of the Amorites.* (Numbers 21:29)

Where there is wickedness in the heart of the leaders:

> *Woe unto the wicked! it shall be ill with him: for the reward of his hands shall be given him.* (Isaiah 3:11)

> *And it came to pass after all thy wickedness, woe, woe unto thee! saith the Lord GOD.* (Ezekiel 16:23)

When leaders are given to worldliness or worldly enjoyments:

> *Do not love the world or the things in the world. If anyone loves the world, the love of the Father is not in him.* (1 John 2:15)

> *You adulterers! Don't you realize that friendship with the world makes you an enemy of God? I say it again: If you want to be a friend of the world, you make yourself an enemy of God.* (James 4:4)

> *Who has woe? Who has sorrow? Who has contentions? Who has complaints? Who has wounds without cause? Who has redness of eyes? Those who linger long at the wine, Those who go in search of mixed wine.* (Proverbs 23:29–30)

> *Woe unto them that rise up early in the morning, that they may follow strong drink; that continue until night, till wine inflame them!* (Isaiah 5:11)

> *Woe unto them that are mighty to drink wine, and men of strength to mingle strong drink.* (Isaiah 5:22)

When leadership is built around individuals rather than a team or the people:

> *For if they fall, the one will lift up his fellow: but woe to him that is alone when he falleth; for he hath not another to help him up.* (Ecclesiastes 4:10)

When leaders are men without capacity, stable character, and are lazy:

> *Woe to thee, O land, when thy king is a child, and thy princes eat in the morning!* (Ecclesiastes 10:16)

When leaders allow or backup rights of people that are against the Lord's to thrive in the land:

> *The shew of their countenance doth witness against them; and they declare their sin as Sodom, they hide it not. Woe unto their soul! for they have rewarded evil unto themselves.* (Isaiah 3:9)

When leaders corner the wealth and resources meant to alleviate the suffering of the lead unto themselves and continually impoverish them:

> *Woe unto them that join house to house, that lay field to field, till there be no place, that they may be placed alone in the midst of the earth!* (Isaiah 5:8)

When leaders and the lead are increasingly transgressing and trespassing against the divine dictates of truthfulness, righteousness, purity, selflessness, justice and uprightness, Godliness, and service:

> *Woe unto them that draw iniquity with cords of*
> *vanity, and sin as it were with a cart rope.* (Isaiah 5:18)

When leaders are not just or are not upholding justice without respect of anyone:

> *Woe unto them that call evil good, and good evil;*
> *that put darkness for light, and light for darkness; that*
> *put bitter for sweet, and sweet for bitter!* (Isaiah 5:20)

When leaders rely on their human wisdom: their experience, educational knowledge, academic qualifications, and repulsive to divine leading and wisdom:

> *Woe unto them that are wise in their own eyes,*
> *and prudent in their own sight!* (Isaiah 5:20)

When the people exalt leaders that God debased:

> *Then said I, "Woe is me! for I am undone;*
> *because I am a man of unclean lips, and I dwell in*
> *the midst of a people of unclean lips: for mine eyes*
> *have seen the King, the LORD of hosts."* (Isaiah 6:5)

When unrighteousness and treachery are the pillars of leadership:

> *Woe unto them that decree unrighteous*
> *decrees, and that write grievousness which they have*
> *prescribed.* (Isaiah 10:1)

> *From the uttermost part of the earth have*
> *we heard songs, even glory to the righteous. But I*

said, *"My leanness, my leanness, woe unto me! the treacherous dealers have dealt treacherously; yea, the treacherous dealers have dealt very treacherously."* (Isaiah 24:16)

Woe to thee that spoilest, and thou wast not spoiled; and dealest treacherously, and they dealt not treacherously with thee! when thou shalt cease to spoil, thou shalt be spoiled; and when thou shalt make an end to deal treacherously, they shall deal treacherously with thee. (Isaiah 33:1)

When leaders are proud:

Woe to the crown of pride, to the drunkards of Ephraim, whose glorious beauty is a fading flower, which are on the head of the fat valleys of them that are overcome with wine! (Isaiah 28:1)

When leaders love darkness and its works than being transparent and accountable to God and the lead:

Woe unto them that seek deep to hide their counsel from the LORD, and their works are in the dark, and they say, Who seeth us? and who knoweth us? (Isaiah 29:15)

When leaders take counsels that are against the ways and desires of God:

Woe to the rebellious children, saith the LORD, that take counsel, but not of me; and that cover with a covering, but not of my spirit, that they may add sin to sin. (Isaiah 30:1)

When leaders seek for help from people and mediums that are rejected by God or push God aside in their leadership activities:

> *Woe to them that go down to Egypt for help; and stay on horses, and trust in chariots, because they are many; and in horsemen, because they are very strong; but they look not unto the Holy One of Israel, neither seek the LORD!* (Isaiah 31:1)

When leaders put themselves in God's position and act like they are indispensable:

> *Woe unto him that striveth with his Maker! Let the potsherd strive with the potsherds of the earth. Shall the clay say to him that fashioneth it, What makest thou? or thy work, He hath no hands?* (Isaiah 31:1)

When leaders have no respect for the elderly and deliberately look down on them:

> *Woe unto him that saith unto his father, What begettest thou? or to the woman, What hast thou brought forth?* (Isaiah 45:10)

When the leaders are murderers, destiny's destroyers, future bleakers, and violent:

> *For I have heard a voice as of a woman in travail, and the anguish as of her that bringeth forth her first child, the voice of the daughter of Zion, that bewaileth herself, that spreadeth her hands, saying, "Woe is me now! for my soul is wearied because of murderers."* (Jeremiah 4:31)

When leaders laid no foundation for prosperity of their people for the benefit and preseverance of a greater future:

> *Blessed are those who fear to do wrong, but the stubborn are headed for serious trouble. A wicked ruler is as dangerous to the poor as a roaring lion or an attacking bear. A ruler with no understanding will oppress his people, but one who hates corruption will have a long life. A murderer's tormented conscience will drive him into the grave. Don't protect him! The blameless will be rescued from harm, but the crooked will be suddenly destroyed.* (Proverbs 28:14–18)

When leaders do not lead men to God but consent to every form of ungodliness in order to protect the rights of their people:
How can you justify the wicked and stand up for the devil rather than God? How can you call what goes against God's Word good? How can you love what God hates? Whose side are you on?

> *Woe to those who call evil good and good evil, who put darkness for light and light for darkness, who put bitter for sweet and sweet for bitter.* (Isaiah 5:20)

> *Have nothing to do with the fruitless deeds of darkness, but rather expose them. It is shameful even to mention what the disobedient do in secret.* (Ephesians 5:11–12)

When leaders are idolatrous:

> *I have seen thine adulteries, and thy neighings, the lewdness of thy whoredom, and thine abomi-nations on the hills in the fields. Woe unto thee, O Jerusalem! wilt thou not be made clean? when shall it once be?* (Jeremiah 13:27)

Woe unto him that saith to the wood, "Awake; to the dumb stone, Arise, it shall teach! Behold, it is laid over with gold and silver, and there is no breath at all in the midst of it." (Habakkuk 2:19)

Woe to the idol shepherd that leaveth the flock! the sword shall be upon his arm, and upon his right eye: his arm shall be clean dried up, and his right eye shall be utterly darkened. (Zechariah 11:17)

When leaders amass riches through unrighteous means:

Woe unto him that buildeth his house by unrighteousness, and his chambers by wrong; that useth his neighbour's service without wages, and giveth him not for his work. (Jeremiah 22:13)

When leaders have no temperament that keep people together but create a tense atmosphere that breeds discomfort, distress, and chaos:

Woe be unto the pastors that destroy and scatter the sheep of my pasture! saith the LORD. (Jeremiah 23:1)

Where sin abounds in leadership and among the lead; both the leaders and the people have become stiff-hearted and impudent:

The crown is fallen from our head: woe unto us, that we have sinned! (Lamentations 5:16)

Woe to them that devise iniquity, and work evil upon their beds! when the morning is light, they practise it, because it is in the power of their hand. (Micah 2:1)

Woe to her that is filthy and polluted, to the oppressing city! (Zephaniah 3:1)

Where leaders lean on their own understanding:

> *Thus saith the Lord GOD, "Woe unto the foolish prophets, that follow their own spirit, and have seen nothing!"* (Ezekiel 13:3)

> Thus says the LORD, *"Cursed is the man who trusts in man And makes flesh his strength, Whose heart departs from the LORD."* (Jeremiah 17:5)

Where a nation thrives by violence, lies, robbery of joint patrimonies, and shedding of innocent blood:

> *Wherefore thus saith the Lord GOD, "Woe to the bloody city, to the pot whose scum is therein, and whose scum is not gone out of it! bring it out piece by piece; let no lot fall upon it."* (Ezekiel 24:6)

> *Therefore thus saith the Lord GOD, "Woe to the bloody city! I will even make the pile for fire great."* (Ezekiel 24:6)

> *Woe to the bloody city! It is all full of lies and robbery; the prey departeth not.* (Nahum 3:1)

> *Woe to him that buildeth a town with blood, and stablisheth a city by iniquity!* (Habakkuk 2:12)

Where leaders are self-centered and are without consideration for the welfare of their people:

> *Son of man, prophesy against the shepherds of Israel, prophesy, and say unto them, Thus saith the Lord GOD unto the shepherds; Woe be to the shepherds of Israel that do feed themselves! Should not the shepherds feed the flocks?"* (Ezekiel 34:2)

Where leaders trust in other gods or a mortal or a medium or prefer other sources of power:

> *Woe to them that are at ease in Zion, and trust in the mountain of Samaria, which are named chief of the nations, to whom the house of Israel came!* (Amos 6:1)

Where leaders use their power to impoverish people for their enrichment:

> *Shall not all these take up a parable against him, and a taunting proverb against him, and say, Woe to him that increaseth that which is not his! how long? and to him that ladeth himself with thick clay!* (Habakkuk 2:6)

When leaders are covetous to get to the top:

> *Woe to him that coveteth an evil covetousness to his house, that he may set his nest on high, that he may be delivered from the power of evil!* (Habakkuk 2:9)

A nation is doomed when her leaders are agents of woes, or in other words, when leadership provided is contrary to God's preference. When a leader is a man after God's heart, he/she will be standing for God before men to raise awareness in the land and influence the lead in the best way to go toward God.

When wrong people are in position of authority, even the righteous may not be spared from their negative consequential influences.

A nation will invariably end up with the kind of leadership it deserves. The book of Isaiah 24: 2 says: "…*And it shall be, as with the people, so with the priest; as with the servant, so with his master; as with the maid, so with her mistress; as with the buyer, so with the seller; as with the lender, so with the borrower; as with the taker of usury, so with the giver of usury to him.*"

And in Jeremiah 5:31, *"The prophets prophesy falsely, and the priests bear rule by their means; and my people love to have it so: and what will ye do in the end thereof?"*

Though leaders are being held more accountable by God, He also holds people they preside over responsible; God disciplines people for following false leaders.

Therefore, since every nation rises or falls by leaders, it is everyone's obligation to discern proper leadership. The leadership one follows is going to govern what you are and who you are; in other words, one will rise or fall depending on the leadership being followed.

One way to tell godly leaders from wicked leaders is to determine if they reach for *responsibility* or *authority*.

Leaders who reach for responsibility are good leaders, while those who seek authority are bad leaders.

A responsive leader considers his position a privilege and opportunity from God that must not be abused serving people, care for them, and put their welfare ahead of his/her own personal interest.

Apostle Paul writes about Timotheus, a responsible leader:

> *But I trust in the Lord Jesus to send Timotheus shortly unto you, that I also may be of good comfort, when I know your state. For I have no man like-minded, who will naturally care for your state.*
>
> *For all seek their own, not the things which are Jesus Christ's. But ye know the proof of him, that, as a son with the father, he hath served with me in the gospel. Him therefore I hope to send presently, so soon as I shall see how it will go with me.*
> (Philippians 2:19–23)

Bad leaders use their position to lord themselves over people; they exercise autocratic powers over their subjects and are never ready to meet the aspiration of God and men in leadership.

Bad leaders care less about others except themselves; they surround themselves with people who are willing to tell them what they want to hear and who will only run with their selfish agenda.

Authority in Leadership

No source of any leadership authority is more ancient than God's who was before the beginning and will remain to the end.

Where a leader derives his authority will tell where his loyalty is and how best or worst, he will govern.

> *Apostle Peter admonishes leaders whose interest to seek authority in 1 Peter 5:2–3 as follows:*
> *…Feed the flock of God which is among you, taking the oversight thereof, not by constraint, but willingly; not for filthy lucre, but of a ready mind; Neither as being lords over God's heritage, but being ensamples to the flock.*

Where and how a leader derives his/her authority will determine who and what he/she will be loyal to, what to expect of his/her leadership, what will be treasurable to him, where his heart will be, the kind of leadership he will provide, where he will place God, and how he will see and comprehend God in leadership.

The Bible says you are a servant to whom you yield yourself to obey; a servant cannot be greater than his master—the means by which a leader emerges will either hunt him or pave way for his greatness.

Whether a leader is selected or appointed or elected, if the authorship of his leadership is not godly inspired or authorized or premised first on being accountable to God, the leader is bound to do the biding of those who choose him while violating God's demands for leading men.

It is very true that God uses men to accomplish His goals, but not all those men desire or root for or prefer are aligned to the dictates of God in leadership.

> The means by which a leader emerges will
> either hunt him or pave way for his greatness.

God will never promote righteousness in unrighteousness as long as there is a foundational error in how leaders emerge. God is too critical about how one is heralded into leadership than his abilities. Even in a case where the emerged leader is a child of God, the process of his/her ascendance is first weighed on the scale of right or wrong.

There are four levels of authority in practice. They are delegated authority, stipulative authority, authority of custom or tradition, and functional authority.

Delegated authority: proceeds from responsibility one is saddled with and never extend beyond one's responsibility in leadership. It is the authority to represent another and do as he would if present.

The awareness of all leaders in any position to the fact that they are standing in for God in the midst of people will make them to exercise restrains and lead with the fear of God. They will also place God in position above any other individual(s) who might have been instrumental to their emergence. Every leader has responsibility to God first, though toward men.

Apostle Paul admonishes that, *"Obey them that have the rule over you, and submit yourselves: for they watch for your souls, as they that must give account, that they may do it with joy, and not with grief: for that is unprofitable for you"* (Hebrews 13: 17).

The word *rule* does mean leadership by ruthless dictatorship or forcing of one's will on others but also to give shepherd-like leadership.

Nearly all men in leadership are indirectly authorized to stand in for God because only He bears rule in the affairs of men. All leaders are God's delegates in the affairs of men, and therefore they owe God total submissiveness and allegiance.

Most leaders' allegiance is to men rather than to God because of how they emerge and the fear of losing out, owing to the strength of few people who are in control of public space with enormous power to do and undo.

Jesus called the disciples to Himself and said, *"But ye shall receive power, after that the Holy Ghost is come upon you: and ye shall be witnesses unto me both in Jerusalem, and in all Judaea, and in Samaria, and unto the uttermost part of the earth"* (Acts 1:8).

Jesus delegated the apostles to witness of Him to the world, and so their source of leadership authority does not permit them to bear their own witnesses aside that of Jesus.

Stipulative authority: this authority is derived from contracts or legal agreements between two parties to carry out a specific action based on mutual benefits if fulfilled and penalties if violated.

The case between Jacob and Laban when Jacob desired to marry Rachel in Genesis 29:9–30 is very instructive on stipulative authority. Laban stipulated seven years for Jacob to serving him before he can marry his daughter.

Every leadership that results from contracts and agreements ties the hands of leaders involved with little or without allowance for needful changes, and when the needful changes are critical, there are bound to be misrule, misrepresentation, misdeed, conflicts, and bad leadership.

Except God's verdicts are brought into the terms of contracts and agreements, the danger of misstep in leadership is imminent; deception, lies, and wickedness may dominate the relationship among the players.

Authority of custom or tradition: this authority is derived from established practice accepted in a culture. Though there are good traditions that have proven over years to be for common good, but there are also bad traditions which are conflictual to God's will and position in leadership. There are leaders who are custodians of traditions and customs; they are to preserve the ancient paths of their forefathers among their subjects.

These traditions and cultures, even though they have been in existence a long time ago, not all of them are aligned to the positions of God in administering people. Where leaders in this respect tenaciously hold on to the beliefs that originated from men, there is bound to be confusion, conflicts, and leadership failure in the society because only the ways to live guaranteed by God is impeccable, secured, rooted in truth, and incontrovertible.

The customs and traditions of men cannot sustain them in leadership, nor will it be sufficient to deal with human complexity because over the years, and even as of now, people get wiser and tougher than traditions and customs; and that is why most of them have been set aside, modified, changed, and collapsed.

Except leaders who derive their authority from customs and traditions become more conscious of God's positions in leading men; they will end up working against God while upholding the doctrines and beliefs of men that are not only inimical to their peaceful existence but run afoul of God's laws, commands, and statutes.

No source of any leadership's authority is more ancient than God's who was before the beginning and who will remain at the end.

And the days which Jeroboam reigned were two and twenty years: and he slept with his fathers, and Nadab his son reigned in his stead. (1 Kings 14:20)

The book of Mark 7:8–9 says, *"For laying aside the commandment of God, ye hold the tradition of men, as the washing of pots and cups: and many other such like things ye do. And he said unto them, Full well ye reject the commandment of God, that ye may keep your own tradition."*

Some of the sources of human traditions and customs are not God's, nor are they in compliance with the Word of God. There are cases of traditional practices that are outright evil, for example, there is a custom that demand that a newly installed king in a particular tribe in Nigeria must eat the heart of his late predecessor; so the question is, how can God be party to that evil practice? God's ways to leadership and in leadership are pure, transparent, good, righteous, not fearful, and not destructive. God does not do evil, nor does He tempts man with evil.

> God's ways to leadership and in leadership
> are pure, transparent, good, righteous, not fear-
> ful, and not destructive. God does not do evil,
> nor does He tempts man with evil.

Functional authority: arises from individual's capability and ability. Some of these abilities results from natural endowment by God, through learning and training, through God's divine enablement, and through experience or schools of hard knocks.

Jesus recognized functional authority when he said, *"But when Jesus heard that, he said unto them, They that be whole need not a physician, but they that are sick"* (Matthew 9:12).

And it was Peter He sent to catch fish in Matthew 17:24–27 to pay tribute.

The common means by which leaders emerge and derive leadership authority include elections, selections, appointments, and cultural and traditional customs which also include family and parental consents, natural order, and self-emergence which is a function of individual's determination and vision. But most importantly, it is by divine providence—which if it is not the root through which a leader emerges, the leader may end up as a disaster.

The books of Psalms and Daniel say:

> *For promotion cometh neither from the east,*
> *nor from the west, nor from the south.* (Psalm 75:6)

The word *promotion* means "elevation into higher office of responsibilities" or "being considered as a qualified person for an exalted position."

> *This matter is by the decree of the watchers,*
> *and the demand by the word of the holy ones: to*

the intent that the living may know that the most High ruleth in the kingdom of men, and giveth it to whomsoever he will, and setteth up over it the basest of men. (Daniel 4:17)

Daniel answered and said, "Blessed be the name of God for ever and ever: for wisdom and might are his: And he changeth the times and the seasons: he removeth kings, and setteth up kings: he giveth wisdom unto the wise, and knowledge to them that know understanding:" (Dan 2:20–21)

The Immutable Truth on Leadership in the Bible

The immutability of God transcends the rigors, complexities, failures, and responsibilities of leadership among men.

Only the immutable, infallible, irrefutable, and endless God can tell and define what the truth is in leadership.

The truth from a mortal man is a function of who he is. Every man is limited and is not in the knowledge of all things. Sometimes he thinks less of what is necessary and important to focus on triviality. His ways are not exact because there is a struggle between his inner being and the desires of the outer man.

He is emotional and, most times, finds it difficult to separate his emotional judgement from the fixed statues and judgement of God.

Though his humanity always lay demands on nature, he goes wrong many times to get what is needed. In the fullness of man, he is being prone to mistakes and errors which may lead to critical losses. He is not infallible, nor is he sufficient of himself/herself.

What a man holds on to as the truth are contestable by other people, but only the truth from God is undeniable, incontestable, unchangeable, and valid for every generation from everlasting to everlasting.

The verdicts of God on leadership are true to all generations. His immutable truth on leadership is the panacea for delivering human race from all problems that are ravaging it from nation to nation, people of diverse language, culture, and different belief systems.

1. Men are created in the image of God; therefore, only those who have submitted to God's leadership can lead others successfully.
2. Every creature is conditioned naturally and not by choice to the leading of God for their own good, and for their woes when God's leadership is being rejected.
3. Human capability or natural endowments does not automatically qualify or give a person a place in leadership because no man has what it takes to lead others except by divine enablement.
4. Every leader submits to the authority of the source of his leadership.
5. No one can provide a leadership beyond his belief system, what he values, and everything that defines his personality.
6. The first leadership responsibility is to self and the critical test of self-leadership is self-control.
7. Leadership position over men is hold in trust for God; only God bears rule in the affairs of men.
8. In leadership, men are led to God. The leaders stand for God before men and not for men before God.
9. Whatever is in thy power to do for another person places you in a position of providing leadership.
10. God is never in hurry to choose leaders until He has molded them to be able to bear the debacles of leading men and being able to make themselves of no reputation but ready to give all for servanthood.
11. The principal requirement for leadership is divine wisdom and not compulsorily acquired knowledge, which of course is an enabler of leading with a difference.
12. God raises leaders in every generation to fulfill His purpose for creation. It is the failure of people to identify these

leaders and place them in charge that makes one generation to another to experience defeats, retardation, and retrogression in growth and performance.

13. The will of man, except birthed by the will of God, throws him off-balance in the face of critical leadership tests. It is only God that will in man to do the bidding of providing godly leadership even in the time of weakness, frustration, and rebellion of the lead.

14. Every leader produces his/her kinds. The best of a bad leader is to reproduce more bad leaders, and the least of a good leader is to create an environment for the evolvement and multiplication of generational leaders who uphold at all times the divine mandate for leadership.

15. Everyone has common sense and deploys it in different ways; only men with uncommon sense called "divine sense" have audacity, preparedness, and capabilities to provide leadership in the face of hysteria absurdity.

16. Because life is either fair or unfair, championing a fair course in life for men is a function of leadership provides them.

17. The ruthlessness of providing leadership is in justice, equity, fairness, accountability, honesty, truth, transparency, Godliness, love, and allegiance to God against the unrighteousness of men.

18. Whatever and whoever one is not accountable for in leadership will be a snare unto failing God and men.

19. That one is being showered with praises as a leader by men may not imply an approval as God's choice.

20. The spiritual content of leadership is weightier than its measure in terms of meeting the needs of the lead. Every profit unto men in leadership that does not profit God first will spell doom for them.

21. There are no acceptable leadership norms, cultures, practices, institutional acceptable research, and schools of thoughts that give directions and is upheld in leadership more than the counsels, teachings, and principles of God in ruling in the affairs of men.

22. Homefront is the critical place of providing and demonstrating godly leadership before one emerges with God's approval as a leader of men.

23. The life of a leader is the soil for the seeds planted in leadership must first grow before they germinate in the lives of others.

24. The art of leadership is not dramatic but an outpouring of life of a leader unto men to raise awareness of God and leading them unto prosperity and discovering of who they are for the Lord.

25. The afflictions of men will continue to rise and multiply as long their choice of leaders are rejected by God.

26. The mastery of earthly leadership is conditioned with deceits, manipulations, lies, selfishness, fraudulence, violence, and unrighteousness. Only the divine incursion into the spirit of man can embolden him to lead in the fear of the Lord.

27. The limitedness of a man in leadership obviously forces him to lose strength, become weak, and misses his steps in the time of leadership crises; only the strength of God can bail him out and restore his integrity.

28. There is no impeccable model for leadership than that of Jesus Christ, the Lord and savior of the world. The Spirit of Jesus is the spirit of leadership.

29. If a leader's faithfulness is not total in leading men in the most negligible responsibility, his/her promotion for a bigger assignment will be the undoing of his destiny and that of the lead.

30. Everything has its source; the deliverables of a leader can be traced to where he/she derives his/her leadership authority. The strength of leadership is in the one who ordained a person into it. God's strength is revealed through the weakness of men He chooses as leaders.

31. The unraveling of mysteries of leadership is in the understanding of God and how He wires men: their adaptability, their limits, their strengths, their weaknesses, their thoughts, and how these interplay in their relationship with Him and their fellowmen.

Divine Chastisement in Leadership

When people reject God's leadership providence, it is either they end up consuming themselves or cause God to raise cruel leaders that will chastise them so that they can return to Him.

Can the rush grow up without mire? can the flag grow without water? Whilst it is yet in his greenness, and not cut down, it withereth before any other herb. So are the paths of all that forget God; and the hypocrite's hope shall perish. (Job 8:11–13)

But their demand displeased Samuel when they said, "Give us a king to judge and rule over us." So Samuel prayed to the Lord. The Lord said to Samuel, "Listen to the voice of the people in regard to all that they say to you, for they have not rejected you, but they have rejected Me from being King over them. Like all the deeds which they have done since the day that I brought them up from Egypt even to this day—in that they have abandoned (rejected) Me and served other gods—so they are doing to you also." (1 Samuel 8:6–8)

The divine purpose of earthly government or leadership is to suppress evil or put it in check in order for citizens to live in peace and be at rest from every influence that may purportedly lead them away from God and subject them to servitude.

OKESOLA MOSES OLUSOLA

God is unrepentantly committed to meeting the needs of all men through leadership provided to them, but when God's leadership is rejected; when the governed sets aside God and rejoices in ungodliness; when there is so much wickedness in the land; when a nation or a country, or a people becomes arrogant and rebellious against God; when men decide what is good for them at the expense of God's eternal truth; when the people that sit in judgement call evil good and good evil; when the source of authority over the people God created to dominate the world is satanic, then God has a way of humbling them by allowing bad leaders and ungodly persons to reign over His people so that they may learn their lessons through hard ways in order to come to repentance.

God's position on leadership is that foreigners or strangers are not permitted to rule over Israel; His desire is never to allow miscreants, the wicked and ungodly men to bear rule over any nation in the world but the righteous except they put their hands in sin.

> *When you enter the land the LORD your God is giving you and have taken possession of it and settled in it, and you say, "Let us set a king over us like all the nations around us, be sure to appoint over you a king the LORD your God chooses. He must be from among your fellow Israelites. Do not place a foreigner over you, one who is not an Israelite."* (Deuteronomy 17:14–15)

> *For the scepter of wickedness shall not rest On the land allotted to the righteous, Lest the righteous reach out their hands to iniquity.* (Psalm 125:3)

God chastises every nation of people that has no regard for Him or His words or refuses His choice of leaders.

> The book of Joshua 2:12–15 says, *"Then the Israelites did evil in the sight of the LORD and worshiped and served the Baals, and they abandoned the*

> LORD, *the God of their fathers, who brought them out of the land of Egypt. They followed other gods from the gods of the peoples who were around them, and they bowed down to them, and offended and provoked the* LORD *to anger. So they abandoned the* LORD *and served Baal [the pagan god of the Canaanites] and the Ashtaroth. So the anger of the* LORD *burned against Israel, and He gave them into the hands (power) of plunderers who robbed them; and He sold them into the hands of their surrounding enemies, so that they could no longer stand [in opposition] before their enemies. Wherever they went, the hand of the* LORD *was against them for evil (misfortune), as the* LORD *had spoken, and as the* LORD *had sworn to them, so that they were severely distressed."*

Whenever a nation or people overrides God's right over them and creates and establishes theirs, God always allows their enemies to reign over them; He does that to prove to them that "He is the one that rules in the affairs of men," and to secure their attention in repentance.

Prophet Jeremiah was asked to inquire of the Lord concerning the war Nebuchadnezzar, king of Babylon, made against Israel, and this is what he said:

> For thus says the Lord, *"Behold, I will make you a terror to yourself and to all your friends; they will fall by the sword of their enemies while you look on. And I will give all Judah into the hand of the king of Babylon; he will carry them away to Babylon as captives and will slaughter them with the sword. Moreover, I will hand over all the riches of this city, all the result of its labor, all its precious things; even all the treasures of the kings of Judah I will hand over to their enemies, and they will plunder them, and take them away and carry them to Babylon. And you, Pashhur, and all who live in your*

house will go into captivity; you will go to Babylon, and there you will die and be buried, you and all your friends to whom you have falsely prophesied." (Jeremiah 20:4–6)

The reign of the king of Babylon over Israel because of their disobedience and rejection of God's words and leadership He provided them was a devastated experience for Israelites. Strangers ruled over them even in their cities and were scattered over many nations as slaves because of their choices against His.

Highlights of divine chastisement when people reject God and His leadership:

- Strangers become stronger than the citizens.

   The stranger who lives among you will rise above you higher and higher, and you will go down lower and lower. He will lend to you [out of his affluence], but you will not lend to him [because of your poverty]; he will be the head, and you the tail. (Deuteronomy 28:43–44)

- Become subservient to their enemies who indirectly bear rule over them.

   You will therefore serve your enemies whom the LORD sends against you, in hunger and in thirst, in nakedness and in lack of all things; and He will put an iron yoke [of slavery] on your neck until He has destroyed you. (Deuteronomy 28:48)

- Experiencing lack in the midst of plenty and economic woes.

   You will bring out a great quantity of seed to the field, but you will gather in little, because the locusts will consume it. You will plant vineyards and cultivate them, but you will not drink the wine or gather the grapes, because the worm will eat them. You will have olive trees throughout your territory but you will not anoint yourselves with the oil, because your olives will drop off. (Deuteronomy 28:38–40)

- There will be cruelty of higher dimension against each other as a result of the oppression of the enemies.

  The man who is most refined and well-bred among you will be cruel and hostile toward his brother and toward the wife he cherishes and toward the rest of his children who remain, so that he will not give even one of them any of the flesh of his children which he will eat, because he has nothing else left during the siege and the misery by which your enemy will oppress you in all your cities.
  The most refined and well-bred woman among you, who would not venture to set the sole of her foot on the ground because she is so delicate and pampered, will be cruel and hostile toward the husband she cherishes and toward her son and daughter, and toward her afterbirth that comes from between her legs and toward the children whom she bears; for she will eat them secretly for lack of anything else, during the siege and the misery by which your enemy will oppress you in your cities. (Deuteronomy 28:54–57)

- The ungodly are raised to execute God's judgment over disobedient nation.

  The burden which Habakkuk the prophet did see. O LORD, how long shall I cry, and thou wilt not hear! even cry out unto thee of violence, and thou wilt not save! Why dost thou shew me iniquity, and cause me to behold grievance? for spoiling and violence are before me: and there are that raise up strife and contention. Therefore the law is slacked, and judgment doth never go forth: for the wicked doth compass about the righteous; therefore wrong judgment proceedeth.

Behold ye among the heathen, and regard, and wonder marvellously: for I will work a work in your days, which ye will not believe, though it be told you.

For, lo, I raise up the Chaldeans, that bitter and hasty nation, which shall march through the breadth of the land, to possess the dwelling places that are not theirs. They are terrible and dreadful: their judgment and their dignity shall proceed of themselves. (Habakkuk 1:1–7)

Though God's intention was not to subject His people to bondage, but by their choices of leaders and flagrant deviance from His ways, He allows them to run themselves aground or learn the hard way to repent from their disobedience.

Despite that God told the Israelites who King Saul would be as captured in 1 Samuel 8:4–20, their desire burned like wildfire until they had their ways. But in the long run, they asked God for mercy after they had repented from their disobedience, and He forgave them and pleaded their cause.

Even in God's wrath, His love for mankind always plays out to show them mercies and grace for total recovery of all they have lost in an immeasurable manner.

Therefore say thou unto them, "Thus saith the LORD of hosts; 'Turn ye unto me,' saith the LORD of hosts, 'and I will turn unto you,' saith the LORD of hosts." (Zechariah 1:3)

In other words, God forgives the wrongs of His people if they genuinely repent of their ways and give God His uncontestable place in their midst.

The nation of Israel in the Bible time was in bondage and slavery under the ruthless leadership of Pharaoh because of their flagrant disobedience unto God. And after they have cried unto God and repented of their sins, God raised Moses—a deliverer, a leader after His heart—to restore their dignity.

> *And the LORD said, "I have surely seen the affliction of my people which are in Egypt, and have heard their cry by reason of their taskmasters; for I know their sorrows; And I am come down to deliver them out of the hand of the Egyptians, and to bring them up out of that land unto a good land and a large, unto a land flowing with milk and honey; unto the place of the Canaanites, and the Hittites, and the Amorites, and the Perizzites, and the Hivites, and the Jebusites. Now therefore, behold, the cry of the children of Israel is come unto me: and I have also seen the oppression wherewith the Egyptians oppress them. Come now therefore, and I will send thee unto Pharaoh, that thou mayest bring forth my people the children of Israel out of Egypt."* (Exodus 3:7–10)

When a nation becomes afflicted through leadership appointed to them as a result of her violation of God's eternal providence on how everyone should live, there will be chaos and problems. It will take a nation acknowledgement of her sins and their confession and repentance from them to secure the mercies of God.

> *If we confess our sins, he is faithful and just to forgive us our sins, and to cleanse us from all unrighteousness.* (1 John 1:9)

In conclusion, it won't be easy for a people and a nation that forgets God. The woes that besiege many nations in the world may not only due to the choice of bad leaders, but it is also possible that God allows bad leaders to chastise them because of their unrepentant and stone-hearted stands against His counsels.

Every nation that forgets God or ignores Him in her affairs will cause people more pains than good (Psalm 9:17; Deuteronomy 9:7–8, 4:23, 18:9–13, 12:29–31; 2 Kings 17:14–17, 38; Nehemiah 9:16; Job 8:13; Jeremiah 2:1–37).

The Day of Reckoning

For God shall bring every work into judgment, with every secret thing, whether it be good, or whether it be evil. (Ecclesiastes 12:14)

E very activity of men shall be laid bare open before the Lord in the last day when all things shall be brought into judgment.

Every responsibility a man discharged on earth directly or indirectly will receive the verdict of God. The role being played by individuals in the life of others will be questioned whether it upheld men in God or not.

The deployment of authority everyone has over others will be subjected to the tenets of godly leadership and how well or not it added values to the lives of men.

Are you a parent? Are you a man or a woman who occupies positions in private or public institution? Are you a political leader, a minister of God, a tutor, a community leader, or someone in jurisdiction of power? God will judge what you have done with the destinies of men tied to your life by providing leadership for them.

> You may juggle human laws, you may fool with human courts, but there is a judgment to come, and from it there is no appeal. (Gifford)

> Truly at the Day of Judgment we shall not be examined on what we have read, but what we

have done; not how well we have spoken, but how religiously we have lived. (Kempis)

The day of judgment or the day of reckoning, for which the word *judgment* alone is sometimes used, is that great day at the end of the world and of time when Christ shall sit as judge over all the universe, and when every individual of the human race will be judged and recompensed according to his/her works, whether they be good or evil.

The time of Christ's coming and duration are known only to God. It will break upon the world suddenly and with a glorious but awful majesty. It will witness the perfect vindication of all the ways of God.

The revelation of God's justice, appalling but unstained, will fill the universe with approving wonders.

> *Blow ye the trumpet in Zion, and sound an alarm in my holy mountain: let all the inhabitants of the land tremble: for the day of the LORD cometh, for it is nigh at hand;*
>
> *A day of darkness and of gloominess, a day of clouds and of thick darkness, as the morning spread upon the mountains: a great people and a strong; there hath not been ever the like, neither shall be any more after it, even to the years of many generations.*
>
> *A fire devoureth before them; and behind them a flame burneth: the land is as the garden of Eden before them, and behind them a desolate wilderness; yea, and nothing shall escape them. The appearance of them is as the appearance of horses; and as horsemen, so shall they run. Like the noise of chariots on the tops of mountains shall they leap, like the noise of a flame of fire that devoureth the stubble, as a strong people set in battle array.*
>
> *Before their face the people shall be much pained: all faces shall gather blackness. They shall run like mighty men; they shall climb the wall like*

men of war; and they shall march every one on his ways, and they shall not break their ranks:

Neither shall one thrust another; they shall walk everyone in his path: and when they fall upon the sword, they shall not be wounded. They shall run to and fro in the city; they shall run upon the wall, they shall climb up upon the houses; they shall enter in at the windows like a thief.

The earth shall quake before them; the heavens shall tremble: the sun and the moon shall be dark, and the stars shall withdraw their shining. (Joel 2:1–10)

That day shall witness the classification of all mankind into two: all the righteous will be in one, and all the wicked in the other; all that love God in the one, and all that hate him in the other; all that penitently accepted the leadership of Jesus Christ and lived to uphold His leadership's tenets in the affairs of men, and those who did the opposite.

This judgment and separation of a set of people from another will be eternal: the former will reign with Christ and others, who though were men of timber and caliber or less than that in status on earth but failed God in every respect of the reason God created them whether as leaders or in other capacities, will suffer everlasting woes.

Malachi 3:5, Matthew 7:2, and 2 Corinthians 5:10 respectively say,

And I will come near to you to judgment; and I will be a swift witness against the sorcerers, and against the adulterers, and against false swearers, and against those that oppress the hireling in his wages, the widow, and the fatherless, and that turn aside the stranger from his right, and fear not me, saith the LORD of hosts. (Malachi 3:5)

For with what judgment ye judge, ye shall be judged: and with what measure ye mete, it shall be measured to you again. (Matthew 7:2)

For we must all appear before the judgment seat of Christ; that every one may receive the things done in his body, according to that he hath done, whether it be good or bad. (2 Corinthians 5:10)

There is no escape route for any leader who worked against the counsel of God in leading men. The accolade received on earth by unfaithful and wicked leaders who possibly prospered in deceits and manipulations will not escape the judgment of God on the last day. Hebrews 9:27 says, *"And as it is appointed unto men once to die, but after this the judgment."*

It is also very true that the judgement of God may begin with the wicked and unrighteous leaders here on earth. With all they have amassed and power to subjugate the destinies of men, they live without peace, run when no one pursues them, insecure, bring curses upon their household, and may live to see the worst days at their old age.

The Bible says:

But the wicked are like the tossing sea, For it cannot be quiet, And its waters toss up mire and mud. "There is no peace," says my God, "for the wicked." (Isaiah 57:20–21)

"There is no peace for the wicked," says the Lord. (Isaiah 48:22)

For to a person who is good in His sight He has given wisdom and knowledge and joy, while to the sinner He has given the task of gathering and collecting so that he may give to one who is good in God's sight. This too is vanity and striving after wind. (Ecclesiastes 2:26)

You will tread down the wicked, for they will be ashes under the soles of your feet on the day which I am preparing," says the Lord of hosts. (Malachi 4:3)

He does not keep the wicked alive, But gives justice to the afflicted. (Job 36:6)

That when the wicked sprouted up like grass And all who did iniquity flourished, it was only that they might be destroyed forevermore. (Psalm 92:7)

Nothing attracts the wrath of God in leadership than when leaders of His people are deliberately perpetuating evil to frustrate divine purpose in their lives.

"Woe to the shepherds who destroy and scatter the sheep of my pasture!" declares the Lord. Therefore thus says the Lord, the God of Israel, concerning the shepherds who care for my people: "You have scattered my flock and have driven them away, and you have not attended to them. Behold, I will attend to you for your evil deeds, declares the Lord. Then I will gather the remnant of my flock out of all the countries where I have driven them, and I will bring them back to their fold, and they shall be fruitful and multiply. I will set shepherds over them who will care for them, and they shall fear no more, nor be dismayed, neither shall any be missing," declares the Lord. (Jeremiah 23:1–4)

The word of the Lord came to me: Son of man, prophesy against the shepherds of Israel; prophesy, and say to them, even to the shepherds, "Thus says the Lord God: 'Ah, shepherds of Israel who have been feeding yourselves! Should not shepherds feed the sheep? You eat the fat, you clothe yourselves with the wool, you slaughter the fat ones, but you do not feed the sheep. The weak you have not strengthened, the sick you have not healed, the injured you have not bound up, the strayed you have not brought back, the lost you have not sought, and with force and harshness you have ruled them.'" So they were scattered, because there was no shepherd, and they became food for all the wild beasts. (Ezekiel 34:1–8)

Author's Leadership Quotes

The dimension of influencing men makes leadership more spiritual. A real leader must be able to inspire and align the thoughts, soul and the heart/spirit of men in total submission to doing good.

A person who has failed in providing self-leadership lacks enablement for leading others.

Opposing God's will in providing leadership spells doom and creates a perpetual fall for a people and their leaders.

Leaders are only holding their position in trust for God because it is Him that rules in the affairs of men.

The building up and planting of a People and a Nation to take root in leadership is strictly dependent on their total submission to the leading, instructions and guidance of God. (Jeremiah 42:10–17)

Divine leadership is the holy grail of successful management (both material and immaterial); a prosperous nation; a productive system; a peaceful society; and a sustainable positive relationship.

The needs of men are more spiritual than being tangible. However conscious a man is to his needs and striving in life to meet them, he is still limited by reasoning and therefore, remains unsatisfied even when certain needs have been met.

Leadership dynamics are not deterministic; only God can help a leader to navigate through the behavioral unpredictability and complexity of men.

Leading men with their complexity are by divine wisdom and not by instinct. Instinct may be good to view and analyze situations but not in managing lives of men.

Many have worked hard to attain a height in leadership. But when the pursuits of their leadership are against divine purpose, their labors end in vain.

Leadership in error is the one that does not uphold the supremacy of God over all things. Its successes never stand the test and changing demand of time.

It is without understanding, and a great error to think that a man with his inherent complexities can provide leadership for others without divine wisdom. Divine wisdom is the principal need of a leader to succeed and excel in leadership without missing his steps in God.

One shocking revelation in today's leadership is that the unqualified men are not just leaders mostly everywhere but are the deciders of who is fit for leadership.

The Secret of King Asa's leadership was his avowed determination to please the Lord and seek for His direction. (2 Chronicles 14:1–5)

Leadership exploits are not achievable by wishes but by deliberate actions in the knowledge of the place and demand of God in leading men.

A leader who is not accountable to God will always fail the test of transparency.

There is the Spirit of leadership; its source is Jesus. (Isaiah 9:6–7)

A leader not trusted by God will be struggling in providing honorable and profitable leadership.

Whatever a leader is not accountable for will ensnare him, and whosoever he is not accountable to he will not be able to influence positively.

True leadership is more concerned with reorientation, recovery, realignment, and improvement of people than competing with others.

God rules in the affairs of men. Except a leader is God's choice for the people, all his efforts will not profit men.

The two legs of leadership are Capacity and Character. While capacity is a principal requirement, character is what sustains a person in leadership.

Leadership rests on a tripod of God's purpose for man; inherent and developed capacity in him; and godly character building.

It is the leadership role that makes a person a leader and not the position assigns to it.

There is no leader of repute in any part of the world that had led or leading or that may emerge in the space of time triumphantly beyond the understanding he/she has about God's deliberate reason for his/her existence; inmate gifts and talents; burning passions; and relationship with God.

The world as it is today runs with a philosophy that separates leadership at all levels from God's principles in choosing leaders.

The standard sets for leadership through men is characterized with biasness, sentiments, inconsistencies, and self reasonings. Only the metrics or deciding parameters set by God are universal, absolute, right, and true from generation to generation. (2 Corinthians 10:12–18)

Leadership is a divine business and responsibility of some men for the sake of others.

There are different schools of thoughts on leadership; but the greatest book and revelation on it and leaders is the BIBLE. This greatest book has history of types of leaders including the ones chosen by God without concealing their errors, mistakes, and how God chastised them.

There is a very high tendency for a leader to be charismatic, enthusiastic, courageous, and still be morally bankrupt. An immoral leader is not God's choice in providing leadership.

Every leader is limited and insufficient in himself/herself.

The best of human leadership can never be compared to God's choice of men in leadership.

The personality behind leadership is revealed by a Belief System. A leader is a product of what he/she believes.

The leaders who are unrepentant followers of God in total obedience and full commitment can lead others to a secured destination.

A man is a spiritual being whose needs for existence and sustenance are mostly intangible, and only God can meet those needs.

The needs of men are majorly and mostly spiritual; only leaders who have deep relationships with God have what it takes in meeting them.

However conscious a man is to his needs, and striving in life to meet them, he is still limited by reasoning, and therefore, remains unsatisfied when certain needs have been met.

God does not take sides with the majority or minority but agrees with whatever and whoever is just, righteous, pure, and truthful at all times.

The leadership position a person occupies is strictly a function of the assignments/ purpose/divine responsibilities he is created for. When a leader occupies a position God did not wire him for, his failures and frustrations will know no bound.

A man reasons to meet his needs within the scope of what is possible because many things are indeed impossible unto him, but to God, all things are very possible.

Leadership at all levels is standing for God before men and not for men before God.

Being a leader is not a right or a positional status. Those who are God's choice as leaders are on duty daily given directions where needed.

The capability of a leader and his leadership is measured by how much more can be done with less.

Every leader raised by God leads men to where God wants them to be and not where they want to go.

References

Akanni, Gbile. 2003. *Pathway To Leadership*. Peace House Publications.

Holmes, David L. 2006. *The Faiths of the Founding Fathers*. Oxford University Press. ISBN 978-0-19-530092-5. Retrieved 2012-09-14.

Kincaid, Zach. 2017. https://www.sharefaith.com/blog/2017/02/founding-fathers-of-the-united-states/.

Mullins, Laurie J. 1996. *Management and Organisational Behaviour. Fourth Edition.* Pitman Publishing.

Robbins, Stephen P. 2003. Organizational Behavior. Tenth Edition. Pearson Education.

The Holy Bible.

About the Author

Okesola Moses Olusola is a teacher of God's Word with divine call for significant impact in his generation.

He is totally committed to leadership development, discipleship, and raising of people to occupy every stratum of the society for Christ. He is also coordinating Word Fellowship Outreach and Teens' Leadership Academy.

Moses is a management consultant: a continuous improvement professional, a business process analyst, and a decision analyst.

He is happily married to Douye Felicia, and both are richly blessed with Master Oluwatimilehin Einstein Paul.

He is an ordained pastor for the past fourteen years at CSBM Worldwide, a revival ministry whose vision is "to restore spiritual sight to all who are blinded by all forms of religion and to cancel interference of spiritual blindness."

Lightning Source UK Ltd.
Milton Keynes UK
UKHW020631060323
418093UK00011B/123

9 798886 169492